INCREASE ITS WORTH

101
Ways to
Maximize
the Value
of Your
House

No. 3073
$23.95

INCREASE ITS WORTH

JONATHAN ERICKSON

101
Ways to
Maximize
the Value
of Your
House

TAB BOOKS Inc.
Blue Ridge Summit, PA

FIRST EDITION
FIRST PRINTING

Copyright © 1989 by TAB BOOKS Inc.
Printed in the United States of America

Library of Congress Cataloging in Publication Data

Erickson, Jonathan, 1949-
    Increase its worth.

    Includes index.
    1. Dwellings—Remodeling.   2. House buying.
I. Title.
TH4816.E75   1988   647'.7   88-24818
ISBN 0-8306-9073-5
ISBN 0-8306-9373-4 (pbk.)

TAB BOOKS Inc. offers software for sale. For information
and a catalog, please contact TAB Software Department,
Blue Ridge Summit, PA 17294-0850.

Questions regarding the content of this book
should be addressed to:

    Reader Inquiry Branch
    TAB BOOKS Inc.
    Blue Ridge Summit, PA 17294-0214

Contents

Acknowledgments

I'd especially like to thank Lawrence Smets of the Smets Architectural Group, Irvine, Calif.; Ron Cope of Fleetwood Homes (Worthington, Minn.); John Rugge of New England Homes (Portsmouth, N.H.); Karen Mason of Realty World (Fairfax, Va.); and Sandra Anderson of Great Western Financial (Santa Ana, Calif.). Also, I'd like to thank Larry Wilson of Merillat Industries (Adrian, Mich.); Bob de Camara of Armstrong (Lancaster, Pa.); Nancy Deptolla of Kohler (Kohler, Wis.); and Sharon Dohy of Porcher (Chicago, Ill.).

Introduction

If you're like most people, a house is probably the biggest financial investment you'll ever make. As with anything involving money, you certainly want to be sure that you're doing everything you can to invest your resources wisely and to protect your investment once it's been made. The problem with a house, however, is that you usually don't have any way of knowing how prudent your investment is until you sell the house. By then, of course, it can be too late.

Compounding the problem is the lack of information available that specifically addresses how to maximize the resale value of a house. Even professional real estate agents—the people you usually depend upon the most—often rely upon their own experiences. To fill this void, *Increase Its Worth: 101 Ways to Maximize the Value of Your House* was written as a guide for those who are buying or selling a house and who are concerned about getting the most from their investment. This includes those who will be building new homes (or who are having someone build for them), who are buying existing homes, or who are remodeling. The focus of the book, therefore, is to identify those features that are most preferred by home buyers and to help determine what is important in terms of resale potential.

The buyer preferences discussed in this book are not based on subjective observations. Instead, the information comes from extensive surveys conducted by major real estate companies, home developers, professional building associations, and real estate agents and builders who have shared their real-life experiences and knowledge. It is important to note that, although buyer trends do fluctuate from month to month, they are nonetheless consistent over long periods of time. The information presented in *Increase Its Worth* should remain valid for the life of your home.

Why People Buy Homes

HARDLY ANYONE BUYS A HOME TODAY THINKING IT WILL BE the only one you will ever own. In our mobile society, you expect changes in those things that influence how and where you will live—your job, family, even personal preferences. And because change is expected, your emotional and financial ties to a particular house are generally more fragile than they were a generation or so ago. Surveys by the U.S. Census Bureau and other organizations point out that today's typical American moves from one place to another 11 times in his or her lifetime, up from 3 times in a lifetime just a few generations ago. The short and long of this is that people tend to move from one place to another, buying and selling homes in the process, more often than ever before.

Surveys conducted by the National Association of Realtors and other organizations bear this out, indicating that the typical homeowner stays in a particular house an average of only seven years before selling it and buying another. The reasons why people buy a particular house and why they eventually sell it are numerous, ranging from the need for more space in a house to a hedge against inflation. Most people buy a house knowing full well that they will be selling it in a few years.

Because buying a house is usually the greatest expense and biggest investment most people ever make, it is imperative that every homeowner consider, not only the current value of a house, but its future selling price, called the *resale value*, as well. Clearly what every homeowner hopes for when selling a house is a profitable return on investment. As annual capital gains numbers reflect, it's possible for practically every home seller to make a profit. (Capital gains on single-family home sales nationwide routinely are in excess of $100 billion per year.)

Making a profit on your house isn't a matter of simple greed because, unlike stocks or bonds, if you sell one house, you usually have to buy another house to live in. Considering the rate at which housing prices have risen (over 200 percent in the last two decades alone), selling a house for what you originally paid for it a few years ago won't allow you to buy a comparable house today.

It's also significant that home values aren't comparable across the country. Selling a house for $75,000 in Kansas City won't enable you to buy a house of similar size and style in San Francisco. The median price for homes in California, for example, is over $140,000, while the median price for the rest of the nation overall is about $87,000. (The *median* is a midpoint with an equal number of houses selling for more and for less than this amount.) And some homeowners, particularly those in areas of the country that have been hard-hit by economic decline, are even experiencing *negative equity* or *negative resale values* where their homes are selling for far less than what they originally paid for them.

Number of Houses Sold

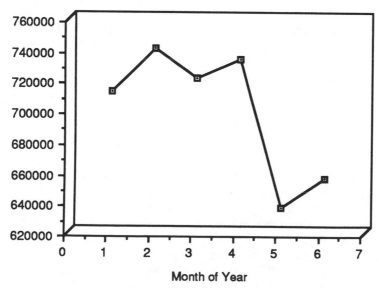

Fig. 1-1. *Monthly sales of single-family homes can fluctuate as evident in the first half of 1987.*

To put some of this into perspective, consider that almost 700,000 single-family homes are sold every month in the United States. According to the U.S. Census Bureau, nearly 5 million homes were sold in the first six months of 1987 alone, as illustrated in Fig. 1-1. Over the past decade, the number of houses sold has risen at the rate of about 38 percent per year. The net result of all these houses being bought and sold is that it has created a housing market that is made up of nearly 60 million owner-occupied homes estimated to be worth perhaps $4 trillion. This continued demand is even more surprising when you consider the consistent, sometimes meteoric rise in housing prices and interest rates.

Accordingly, it is important that homeowners do everything they can to maximize the resale value of their house. What *Increase Its Worth* will do is show you what steps you, as a current or potential homeowner, can take if you are designing, building, buying, or remodeling a house for eventual resale.

PROFILE OF HOME SHOPPERS

By understanding who home shoppers are and what motivates them, you will learn what you can do to make your home more attractive to home buyers and thus maximize your home's resale value. The type of things you need to remember, for example, are that certain kinds of homes tend to appeal to certain kinds of buyers. This section will provide thumbnail sketches of the major categories of home shoppers.

In general, there are three basic categories of home shoppers: first-time buyers, move-up buyers, and move-down buyers. As Fig. 1-2 shows, move-up buyers make up the greatest percentage of home shoppers. In fact, the number of move-up buyers is more than double any other cate-

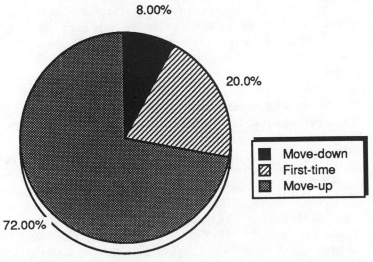

Fig. 1-2. *Categories of home buyers.*

gory of home shoppers. The exact percentages that make up the different categories of shoppers varies from study to study. It is the relative percentages, not the exact figures, that are important.

First-time buyers are young (between 25 and 35 years of age) shoppers who have never owned a house before. Usually, first-timers have saved enough money for the down payment or have borrowed that money from parents. More than 80 percent of first-time buyers are married couples, and about 40 percent of them have children. In two-thirds of the first-buyer households, both spouses have jobs outside the house.

First-time buyers typically have active hobbies; are fitness conscious; like to travel; have savings, investments, and insurance; and own a nearly new car. Because of their numerous outside activities, first-time home buyers often want a smaller house that requires little maintenance and is close to where they work. Coincidentally, a smaller home fits in with their financial capabilities too. The houses that first-time buyers commonly buy often sell for one-third the price of houses bought by move-up buyers. Nearly one-half of these shoppers want homes that conform to their lifestyle. Nonetheless, first-time buyers spend an average of almost $106,000 for a house and saved nearly 2½ years to accumulate the down payment.

Eventually, most first-time buyers hope to become *move-up* (sometimes called *trade-up*) shoppers who purchase larger homes as their needs and financial resources grow. Move-up shoppers often have invested in home improvements, consequently their existing homes tend to be worth more than many more recently built or new homes. As might be expected, move-up buyers also are slightly older (an average of 39 years old) than first-time buyers, have larger families, and make more money. In about two-thirds of all move-up buyer households, both spouses work outside the home.

The final category of home shoppers consists of *move-down buyers*—those families or individuals who, for whatever reasons, are moving from one house to another one that is smaller and less expensive. In many instances, move-down buyers are empty nesters or retirees with adult children who no longer live at home. Therefore, they might not want the four-bedroom house—and all of the cleaning and maintenance that goes with it—like they needed when raising a house full of kids. Alternatively, they move down to a smaller house that requires less maintenance.

Other move-down buyers include individuals or families who have suffered some sort of decline in their standard of living. In these times of economic upheaval and job layoffs, many families simply discover they can't afford the large, extravagant house owned in the good times, and they must sell it to move into something more affordable. In other instances, divorce and other family breakups often cause a dramatic drop in one's standard of living. The result is that partners who split up usually buy two smaller houses that they can afford as individuals instead of the single large house they owned together.

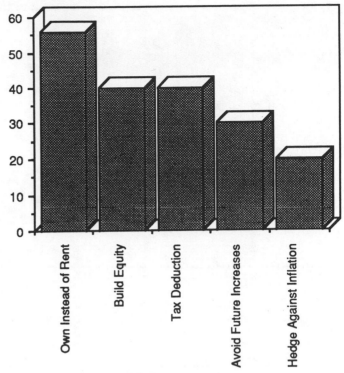

Percentage of Buyers

Fig. 1-3. *Financial reasons for buying a home.*

MOTIVATIONS OF HOME SHOPPERS

While it's easy to say that the primary motivation for buying a house is a desire to fulfill the American dream, there remain numerous concrete reasons why people want to own their own home. One basic motivation is merely to have a place you can call your own, a place you can paint the color you want, a place that reflects who you are. This is the case for a majority of first-time potential buyers, 90 percent of whom rent homes or apartments.

Homeownership offers more tangible benefits, however, especially in terms of financial investment. Over the past few years, homeownership has proven to be one of the most investor-profitable options, consistently providing the greatest, most stable returns on investment. Over a recent 10-year period, investments in housing appreciated at rates three to four times greater than that of standard savings accounts and bonds yields, and approximately five to eight times greater than stocks. The realized capital gains on existing home sales has exceeded the $100 billion mark for a number of years.

As Fig. 1-3 shows, more than 40 percent of the people looking to buy a house see it as a safe way to save money and build equity. About the

Percentage of Buyers

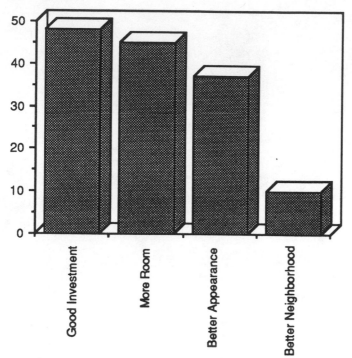

Fig. 1-4. *Important home selection factors.*

same number of people want to take advantage of the tax advantages enjoyed by homeowners, particularly mortgage interest and property tax deductions. In fact, the ability to invest money in a home instead of paying it as rent to a landlord is foremost on the mind of more than 80 percent of first-time buyers. Inasmuch as in many cities rental costs often outstrip monthly payments (particularly when interest rates are down), the biggest problem people have in making the transition from rental to ownership is coming up with the downpayment. As shown in Fig. 1-4, the investment value of a particular home is perhaps the most important yardstick for choosing one house over another for nearly half of the home shoppers. Chapter 2 discusses the investment value of a house in more detail.

Investment value isn't the only reason home shoppers consider buying a specific house, however. Especially among move-up buyers, almost half of the shoppers simply need more room than they currently have. Move-up shoppers want a house with at least 10 percent more floor space than their current home. This additional space is often needed because the family size has grown larger. A need for hobby space and storage also plays a part. A majority of move-up shoppers also suggest

Percentage of Buyers

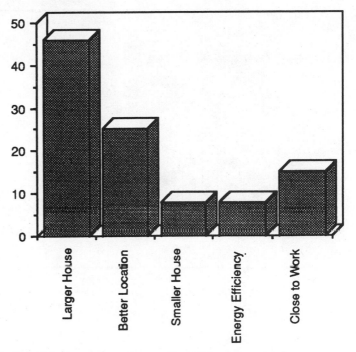

Fig. 1-5. *Nonfinancial reasons for move-up shoppers buying a new home.*

that they would rather have a larger home with fewer features than a smaller home with extensive interior features.

As shown in both Figs. 1-4 and 1-5, many home shoppers, particularly move-up buyers, simply want to move to a different neighborhood. Other reasons for buying a home include the need for a smaller, easier-to-maintain home—particularly among empty nesters or retirees—or a more energy-efficient home. Personal preference as to architectural style and color schemes can also be a factor. Location, both in terms of a specific neighborhood and of a close proximity to work, is also significant.

When weighing the cost of buying a house, most home shoppers are more concerned about the monthly cost or payments for an individual house than they are about its selling price. As Fig. 1-6 illustrates, the overall cost of the house (that is, the selling price plus interest) is more significant to most buyers than the selling price. In fact, a recent survey undertaken by one nationwide real estate company found that the price of a house was the main concern for buyers, surpassing other considerations such as location, neighborhood, and size.

No matter which group of home shoppers you are dealing with and no matter what their individual reasons are for wanting a house, there are several other things that are important to home buyers. Foremost among these is a desire for security and privacy. In a recent Lou Harris

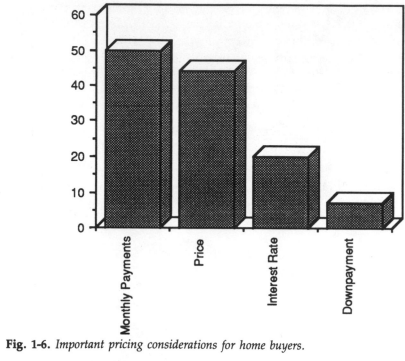

Fig. 1-6. *Important pricing considerations for home buyers.*

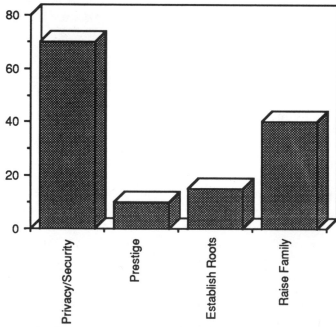

Percentage of Buyers

Fig. 1-7. *Other reasons home buyers have for owning a house.*

poll, more than 93 percent of the home shoppers surveyed indicated that the most significant function of a house was as a sanctuary. People tend to feel more secure if they are in a house that they own. They feel that someone can't make them vacate it as with a rental home, and they feel that they have a greater sense of their own destiny, especially in what they can do with the house. As the chart in Fig. 1-7 illustrates, other reasons for owning a home include the prestige of homeownership and the desire to raise a family in a specific neighborhood and become a greater part of that community.

2

The Importance of Resale Value

A FEW MILES SOUTH OF SAN FRANCISCO IS A HOUSE THAT, over the years, has been dubbed the ''Flintstone house,'' the ''Dome house,'' and even the ''Posh Mud Hut.'' By whatever name the house has gone by (see Fig. 2-1), its owners and local real estate agents have always found it to be difficult to sell, especially at its most recent asking price of just over $500,000. While you might think that price tag is high, consider that the most recent owner lowered the selling price to $500,000 from an original price of slightly more than $750,000, a drop of nearly a quarter of a million dollars, and still found the house hard to sell. (The main reason for the house's high selling price is its location. The average household income is one of the highest in the nation, and most of the houses in the neighborhood sell for more.)

What this example points out is that there is sometimes a big difference between houses that are uniquely individual and those that sell readily. The problem that owners and builders are thus faced with is how to fashion homes that are exceptionally personal while, at the same time, have enough universal charm to appeal to a diverse group of home shoppers.

The original builder of the Flintstone house, for example, was perhaps less concerned about resale values than about building a home that was uniquely his own. For whatever reasons, what he ended up with was a house that antagonized many of his new neighbors and a structure that hasn't been easy to sell. It is also noteworthy that, over the past 10 years, nearby homes have appreciated at a much higher rate than the Flintstone house.

Extraordinary designs aren't the only thing that defines unique homes. Often times, uncommon features within a home make it unique and create selling problems, even when those features are considered attractive by everyone who sees them. That's what one Kansas City homeowner who had a standard, split-level home in a normal subdivision found out when he put up for sale his house that had a beautifully landscaped backyard. Among other features, the backyard included a multitiered rock garden with a recirculating stream and waterfall. While no shoppers denied the beauty of the backyard, what scared them was the maintenance required to keep up the many plants and rock walls. The house eventually did sell, but the homeowner and his realtor estimated that it took perhaps six months to a year longer than normal because of the backyard.

Fig. 2-1. *A unique but somewhat difficult house to sell.*

The Flintstone house certainly isn't the only example of unusual homes that tend to appeal to a narrow segment of the buying market as opposed to the general market as a whole. If you've ever spent a few Sunday afternoons canvassing open houses that are for sale, you probably can compile your own list of designs that are too personal for widespread appeal.

The builder of a particularly unique house in Wisconsin wasn't necessarily attempting to make a statement of one kind or another, but instead was trying to build an economical, energy-efficient home to battle the northern winters. The fact that the underground house was built into a hillside isn't, in itself, exceptional. What makes the house unique, however, is the building material used to construct the house—large, semicircular, metal highway drainage culverts. Figure 2-2 shows what the house looks like. Note the curved roof line. For a number of reasons, this house was on the market more than two years before it eventually was sold at a cost about 25 percent below the original asking price.

In one of the more unusual approaches to building a personal and unique home, one homeowner converted a cave into a 10,000 square foot home, complete with a stalactite ceiling in the living room. The owner

Fig. 2-2. *The exterior of a house built from highway drainage culverts.*

spent more than $1 million to transform the cave into a six-bedroom, four-bathroom tile floor home before he put it on the market. Asking price? About $4 million. So far, serious shoppers have been few and far between.

IS A HOUSE A HOME OR AN INVESTMENT?

The basic question raised by these examples is whether a home is only a roof over your head or an investment in your future. Unless you are a professional builder or real estate developer, your answer is probably yes to both parts of the question. For most homeowners, the home is both a place to live in as convenient and comfortable fashion as possible, and it is a financial investment in the future. What is important to keep in mind is that the investment value of the house only becomes evident when you sell it. If you can't sell the house, or if you have to sell it for less money than you have put into it, then the investment isn't worthwhile. On the other hand, if you are so worried about the value of the house that you are uncomfortable while living there, the investment isn't worthwhile either. Hopefully, you'll be able to establish some equilibrium between the two extremes.

All homeowners are aware of the financial advantages of owning a home—tax write-offs, equity growth, and so on—but few of us are really willing to put off indefinitely all of the basic comforts we need and want today for some economic benefits that we might have sometime in the distant future. Conveniently, a house is one of the few investments in which you can hammer out a balance between today's comforts and tomorrow's financial rewards. (This is one reason why Congress and the Internal Revenue Service have been reluctant to eliminate tax deductions for housing. It also helps explain why deductions for multiple or additional homes have recently been cut back. If the day ever arrives when Congress views housing strictly as an investment vehicle, you can rest assured that homeowners will lose many of the tax benefits they now enjoy.)

There's no question that the financial benefits of homeowning is real. To illustrate this, the National Association of Home Builders cites the example of two similar families (two working parents and one small child) with a $40,000 per year income and each with $10,000 to invest. In the NAHB scenario, one family uses the $10,000 as a downpayment on a $100,000 house and takes on a $90,000 mortgage at 10.5 percent interest. The other family invests their $10,000 in a 10-year Treasury bill paying 5.75 percent interest while continuing to pay $700 per month rent.

After one year, the family that bought the house has a federal income tax bill that is about $1,300 less than the other family. At the same time, the house will have appreciated about $5,000 in value, while the T-bill earned only about $500 in interest. At the end of a 10-year period, the family that owns the house will have paid about $15,000 less in federal taxes than the renters, and the house would likely be valued at over $160,000, or a gain of about $60,000, if it were sold. During the same period, the value of the T-bill would have only increased to slightly less than $18,000. At the same time, the renters would have paid over $100,000 in rent for which they have no return.

Granted, there are many other factors involved—property tax increases, home insurance, maintenance, etc. The bottom line, however, is that homeowners can realize significant investment returns on their property that is not possible for renters.

DETERMINING RESALE VALUE

Assume for the time being that you have a house and are ready to sell it. Short of spending several hundred dollars for a professional appraisal or making a commitment to a real estate agent who might inflate the resale value just to get you to sign a contract, how can you determine what your house is worth? There are two basic methods that professional appraisers use to determine a home's resale value. One method, called the *market* or *sales comparison approach*, essentially compares your property with sales of similar homes in the neighborhood, including homes that have recently been listed for sale or that have actually sold. With the other method, called the *cost approach*, you estimate what it would cost you to buy the land and build the home from scratch. Nevertheless, the only real determining factor is what someone else will pay you for your house, and there are some steps you can take to figure out the market value.

You can begin by taking a look at the assessed value of the house as set by your city or county government property tax department. Use this dollar figure only as a starting point because most local government valuations are usually several years behind the time. If you use this value alone, you might well be significantly underpricing your home.

Once you've determined the lower end value, find out the upper limit of your home's value. To do this, begin asking homeowners who have houses for sale in your neighborhood what they are asking for their homes. Try to stick with houses that are similar to yours so that you are comparing apples to apples. Remember that the home prices they tell you are what they would like to get, probably not what they will get, and that these prices will likely be higher than actual resale values. At the same time, honestly compare your house with those homes. Do those other homes have features that your's does not? Is there any reason why your house should be worth more than other homes?

After you've determined the upper and lower extremes of values, try to establish actual selling values of homes that have recently sold in your neighborhood. This is public information that is usually published in local newspapers. Only in rare instances will you find that the average asking price for a neighborhood is the same as the average selling price. If the newspaper doesn't have a list of the transactions you need, you can go to the county or city recorder's office and dig out the information from records, a job you may find to be time consuming. Another source of the same information might be local real estate agencies, particularly those that subscribe to Multiple Listing Services, which usually tracks housing transactions.

In many cases, real estate agencies will help you establish the market value of your house without you signing a contract that locks up your property with a specific agent. To be sure that the agent is setting an accurate valuation, get estimates from several agents.

While a discussion of for-sale-by-owner homes is largely beyond the scope of this book, the main reason most owners have problems selling their house is because they overprice the property. The basic problem is usually that homeowners are simply too close to the situation and can't make an objective evaluation to set a realistic price. The owner knows what a particular feature originally cost. What he might not be aware of, however, is how much that feature is worth to potential buyers. Some features such as swimming pools, for instance, have installation costs that are much higher than the value added to the home. If you spend $20,000 adding a swimming pool to your house, don't expect that the market value of your home will increase a corresponding amount. Don't be surprised (and, in some cases, feel lucky) if an addition of a feature like a $20,000 swimming pool increases the value of your home only $5,000 or so. This is another reason why you should be aware of the issues surrounding resale values, particularly if you have limited financial resources and want the most for your money.

Real estate and building professionals often speak in terms of the percentage of payback of a home improvement. Assume that in the above example a homeowner has a house worth $100,000, and that owner spends $20,000 adding a swimming pool. That addition doesn't mean that the house is worth $120,000. It might, in fact, increase the value of the house only $5,000 so that the house has a realistic selling price of only $105,000. In this case, the return on investment would be only 25 percent. If the swimming pool increased the value of the house to $110,000, the return would be 50 percent, and so on. When including a special or unique feature to a house, you must consider how much it is worth to you and how much it is worth to someone buying your house. If the convenience of having a swimming pool outside your door is worth $15,000 ($20,000 you pay minus the $5,000 you get back when you sell the house), then by all means put in the pool. Obviously with investments like a swimming pool, the longer you live in the house, the more they tend to pay off. That is, if you live in the house for 15 years, the swimming pool only costs you $1,000 per year; if you stay in the house 5 years, it costs you $3,000 per year. With many home improvements, be happy if you break even on what they cost and what they add to the worth of the house. More importantly, don't forget to account for the intangible convenience and comfort fiscally unprofitable improvements add to your life while you live in the house.

FACTORS THAT AFFECT RESALE VALUES THE MOST

There are several fundamental themes running throughout this book. The basic premise is that virtually no one lives in one house forever and that, eventually, you (or your heirs) must consider the resale value of the home. Another assumption is that it is possible to create a house that satisfies both your personal preferences and the preferences of a broad spectrum of potential buyers. Yet another conjecture is that you do not have unlimited financial resources, and it is important that your investment of that money be as sensible as possible.

Features That Improve Resale Value

As you have seen, there are many factors that play a part in determining the resale value of a home. Table 2-1 shows that the location and condition of the house are significant. The features of a house that real estate professionals consider paramount are the kitchen, bathroom, and master bedroom. So important are these areas that real estate agents refer to them as ''the Big Three.'' The bottom line is that if you have money to invest in your house, you'd be wise to use it to upgrade one of these rooms first. Because of the importance of these rooms, individual chapters of this book are devoted to discussing them in depth. There is a danger of spending too much money for any home feature, even within the Big Three. An extravagant feature that far surpasses basic needs or that causes your house to outshine neighboring homes beyond an acceptable limit will not only make it difficult for you to realize a return on your investment, but it might lower the resale value of the house on the whole.

In addition to enhanced kitchens, bathrooms, and bedrooms, several other key features make wise investments, Table 2-2. One such feature

Table 2-1. Buyer's Primary
Concerns When Considering a House

In Order of Importance:

1.	Price
2.	Location
3.	Neighborhood
4.	Size

Table 2-2. House Features
Most Desired by Buyers

Listed by Frequency of Response:

1.	Fireplace
2.	Large Kitchen
3.	Family Room
4.	Two-car Garage
5.	Sufficient Number of Bathrooms
6.	Master Suite with Bathroom

is the family room. In the Lou Harris poll cited earlier, 99 percent of the home shoppers surveyed said they wanted a home that would be a place to which a family can invite relatives and friends, and a family room is the most convenient place to entertain informally. For remodelers, a renovation that adds a family room can return from 75 to 100 percent of the investment.

Closely tied to the family room is a fireplace. As Table 2-2 shows, virtually every home shopper survey, including those by Great Western Real Estate, Realty World, Chicago Title Insurance, indicate that home shoppers rate fireplaces as a most desirable special feature a house can have. In most instances, the favored location for the fireplace is the family room, although buyers indicate that a fireplace is acceptable in the living room, master bedroom, and even some kitchens.

Especially in cold climates, two-car garages are always good investments, even when buyers only have one car. Not only do garages protect the car from inclement weather, but garages also provide greater security from vandalism and theft. Garages add convenience because you don't have to get out in the snow to clean off the windshield or carry groceries into the house in the rain.

Although less important to buyers than it was in the late 1970s, energy efficiency remains a concern. Houses in extreme climates (hot or cold) need to have double- or triple-pane windows and more than just adequate insulation.

Features That Don't Always Improve Resale Value

A swimming pool has already been mentioned as one special feature that might not return what you originally paid for it. There are two factors, however, that help improve the chances of your gaining a greater return on investment—doing the work yourself and living in the house for a longer length of time.

For example, a common feature many homeowners add to their house is an outside deck. Depending on its size, location, and other factors, a deck commonly adds slightly more than $2,000 to the value of a typical house. It will usually cost you about $3,000 to $4,000 to have a professional carpenter make the addition. If you do the job yourself, it might cost you only about $1,000. The return on investment in this case is at least 200 percent for the do-it-yourselfer, while about 50 percent when someone else builds the deck. The point is that by doing the work yourself, you can significantly lessen the negative impact of many unique or special improvements.

Not all jobs are as easy as a deck addition, however. The quality of workmanship also is very important. A sloppily-built deck will not increase the value of the house and might decrease the value if the buyer sees that it needs work or needs to be torn down.

Generally speaking, any investment that adds less than 50 or 60 percent of what you put in isn't a good investment unless you really like it or unless you live in the house for at least 10 years after adding the feature. In addition to swimming pools, luxury features like attached greenhouses don't add much value, nor do installation of new doors, windows, and skylights. Although they add less than 50 percent of their cost to the value of the house, more efficient windows can provide big savings in energy conservation in extreme climatic regions of the country.

Hot tubs have become a popular special feature in recent years. Depending on the part of the country you live in, however, they only increase your property values at a rate of less than 50 percent of what it costs you to install one.

Special landscaping jobs, like with the house in Kansas City, sometimes stifle buyer interest because of the heavy maintenance required. This is one reason why professional landscaping projects don't provide good returns. Buyers don't want to keep up such a yard themselves, nor do they want to incur the cost of hiring a professional gardener.

SHORT-TERM VERSUS LONG-TERM IMPROVEMENTS

The length of time you live in your house affects the type of special feature improvements you should make. If you plan on being in your house for 10 or 20 years, most of the improvements you make will be justified in terms of immediate comfort and eventual investment return. Such modifications are referred to as *long-term improvements*.

You might plan, however, on being in a house less than 5 years. Perhaps you are only buying a house to fix it up and sell it at a profit before moving up to a larger house. You should be very careful, then, about the kind of renovations you implement. Any features added to the house in this situation might be referred to as *short-term improvements*.

Short-term improvements, sometimes referred to as *cosmetic improvements*, obviously require less time, energy, and money. Just about any part of a house can benefit from being spruced up, and buyers will react favorably to just about any such improvement. The most general (inside and out and in all rooms of the house) and usually the easiest and least expensive short-term improvement you can invest in is a fresh coat of paint. This does more than anything else to impress home shoppers. Not only does fresh paint make a house look cleaner and newer, but it also gives the impression that the current owner (you) cares, and has cared for, the home.

On the outside of your house, for instance, you will want to be sure the door and its surrounding molding has been recently painted so that it looks clean and fresh. Remember, the first and most important impression the buyer has of your house will likely be projected by the front door. Likewise, be sure the front-door light is working and in good repair; replace it, even with an inexpensive fixture, if necessary. At the same time, replace existing house numbers with attractive new numbers that can be easily read from the street.

As the buyer enters your house, he or she should be greeted by freshly painted or resurfaced walls and floors that are free from deep scratches. At the least, be sure all hardwood and tile floors have been waxed; put down a fresh coat of polyurethane on the hardwood floors if necessary. Don't be afraid to replace switch plate and electrical outlet covers with new plates if the old ones are broken, dirty, out of date, or have been painted over. Be sure doorknobs aren't loose; if they are, tighten them up or replace them.

In the kitchen and bathroom, clean and paint (if necessary) cabinet surfaces. Replacing cabinet pulls (knobs) and other hardware is also effective. Clean kitchen appliances inside and out and repaint or touch-up if required. Put a new shower curtain in the bathroom; replace towel bars and other accessories; add a new medicine cabinet.

If you are looking at a house as a short-term investment, avoid major maintenance jobs like reroofing if possible. Obviously, improvements like these will have to be made if there are problems like the roof leaking, but in general, they won't pay off because they simply cost too much money.

If you will be in the house for a while, however, a major maintenance project like reroofing can be an effective long-term improvement. Other worthwhile long-term improvements include upgraded bathrooms, large and feature-filled kitchens, and some attic conversions to functional living space. Include a fireplace addition in profitable, long-term improvements. When all is said and done, however, applications of interior and exterior paint still remains one of the best investments you can make in both short-term and long-term improvements.

3

Design
Strategies

Houses that look good and feel good are houses that sell. Part of what makes a house seem comfortable is the all-around design of the structure and the arrangement of its rooms. If executed appropriately, the design and layout can give a wide variety of home shoppers a sense of warmth that makes the house seem unique and personal, and makes the house easier for you to sell.

Design effectiveness depends on a number of things. The style of some houses, for instance, looks better with large-size structures. The characteristics of the neighborhood in which the house is located is also a factor; some houses might look fine in one neighborhood and inappropriate in others.

A practical, efficient, and flexible floor plan is important not only to your day-to-day comfort, but to the long-range opportunities that exist for selling the house to potential buyers. In addition to defining the positions of the rooms, a floor plan itemizes the relative amount of space, the number of floors, and the general placement of doors, windows, and fixtures (Fig. 3-1).

The design and layout of a house play a greater role than anything else when it comes to determining how much you or someone else likes

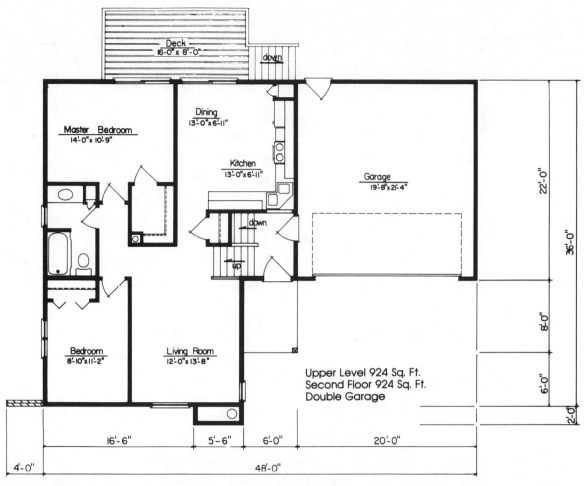

Fig. 3-1. *Sample house floor plan (courtesy of Fleetwood Homes, Inc.).*

a particular house. If the design and layout are not well thoughtout, quality workmanship and expensive fixtures will go unnoticed and not be worth the expense or effort it takes to implement them.

LAYOUT STRATEGIES

When considering what is important about the floor plan of today's homes, think back for a moment to the layout of homes built 100 years ago. At that time, the layout of a house classically consisted of many small rooms that were often closed off in the wintertime. In the summertime, rooms were opened so that air could circulate throughout, creating a more open, but boxy, effect. The overall emphasis was on formality, and the designs were rigid. Homes customarily had a formal dining room and parlor that were used only on special occasions. Specifically in the winter, most of the living actually took place in the kitchen, which was heated

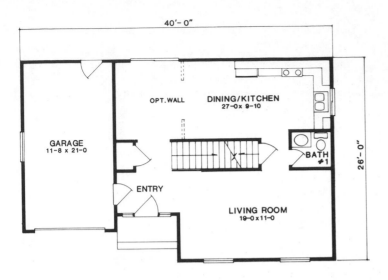

Fig. 3-2. *Open-space floor plan (courtesy of Fleetwood Homes, Inc.).*

by the cooking stove, or in an informal living room. Some rooms of the house were used only two or three days out of the year, while others, such as summer kitchens, enjoyed only seasonal use. Because there was usually enough suitable building land and building costs were relatively low, and because the prevailing tastes of the day dictated such designs, homeowners put up with these somewhat inefficient floor plans.

One of the biggest changes in our society since that time has been an increased acceptance of informal life-styles. People dress more informally today, they interact on a more informal basis, and they generally live more informally as well. Not only has this cultural shift significantly affected the way people dress, it has also had an impact on the layout and floor plan of their homes. In homes that still have formal living and dining areas, for instance, homeowners have found that they rarely use those rooms. Consequently, areas set aside for formal dining and living rooms have been de-emphasized in the floor plan of many new homes. A survey recently conducted by Lou Harris Associates underscores this as 81 percent of the homeowners polled characterized the primary living areas of their home as casual.

This emphasis on informality, which reflects our more casual, mobile life-style, has become the predominant trend in home design over the past few decades. Instead of numerous cubiclelike rooms, today's homes have space that seems to flow in a free-form manner (Fig. 3-2). Space is more open and rooms have multipurpose functions. A large kitchen can easily be adapted to include a dining or family room or, as Fig. 3-3 shows, a living room can include a dining room if the need arises. Not only does this tend to affect our living patterns, but flexible floor plans,

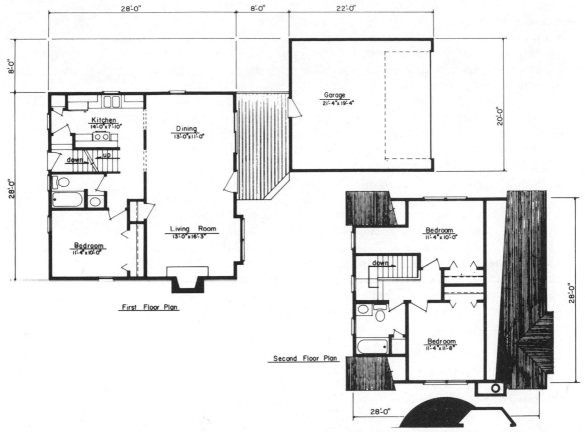

Fig. 3-3. *Floor plan with a flexible living/dining room (courtesy of Fleetwood Homes, Inc.).*

just coincidentally, makes it easier for builders to construct homes that appeal to a wider range of shoppers.

HOUSE ZONES

Even though both the layout of houses and life-styles of the people who live in those houses has changed over the years, a house must still provide the same basic services that it always has. For instance, a house must have group living areas, personal living areas, and service areas.

Group Living Areas

Group living areas consist of those zones within a house where communal or group activities, both leisure and formal, take place. Rooms that fall into this category include living rooms, family rooms, dens, and dining rooms. In many homes, group rooms are designed for specific activities—television watching, reading, conversation, music listening and playing, and so on. Some of these activities might require specialized construction considerations (special wiring for stereos, cable television, personal computers, etc.) or insulation (soundproofing in the case of music).

Smaller homes sometimes have a single living room that is used as the primary recreational group living space in the house. Such an arrangement can become crowded and inconvenient, particularly when a large or growing family is present. When houses are remodeled, a family or recreation room is often the first area added. Because over half of home shoppers say that they need space for family entertainment, a relatively large amount of available floor space can be dedicated for informal family living. On the other hand, fewer than 1 out of 10 say that they definitely need formal entertaining areas. Add the fact that nearly 9 out of 10 home shoppers say that they are spending more time at home in the evenings, and it is easy to see why home builders consider family rooms, in addition to traditional living rooms, a standard feature in new homes.

In many instances, informal living areas are located near and provide access to kitchens and patios, (Fig. 3-4). Layouts such as this make it easier to casually move from one casual environment to another. It also makes it possible for parents, who might be in the kitchen or in the family room, to readily keep an eye on small children as they travel and play inside and outside of the house.

Personal Living Areas

Personal living areas are rooms that are used by no more than one or, at the most, two people at a time. Rooms that fall into this category include

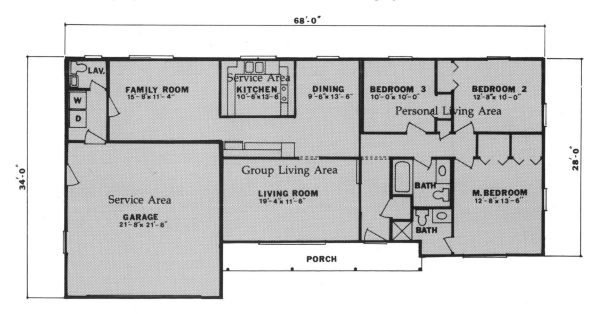

Fig. 3-4. *Living zones within a typical house (courtesy of Fleetwood Homes, Inc.).*

master suites, bedrooms, and bathrooms. In terms of layout, the bedroom is usually one of the simplest rooms in the house. The boxlike appearance of the room is usually interrupted only by a closet and windows. In many ways, creating an efficient and attractive room is therefore often more of a decorating job than one of design. The floor plan of bedrooms typically accentuates privacy, quietness, and comfort, and the rooms are laid out to discourage traffic between rooms.

Master suites, on the other hand, are anything but simple in their layout. Today's master bedrooms often include one or more walk-in closets, full-baths, dressing or sitting areas, and even saunas or spas. It is only fitting that, in many houses, the master suite is the most luxurious area in the house because homeowners typically spend more than one-third of their time in that room alone.

The bathroom is the other personal living area. Unlike the simple bedroom, bathrooms are one of the more complicated and expensive rooms in the house, (Fig. 3-5). Two issues are important when considering

Fig. 3-5. *Today's bathroom with built-in makeup table (courtesy of Merillat Industries, Inc.).*

bathrooms—how many there are and how convenient is their location. Multilevel homes should have a bathroom on each level, while large single-level ranch-style homes probably need a bathroom at each end of the house, particularly if living areas are at one end and bedrooms at the other.

The location of bathrooms, especially in relation to bedrooms and family rooms, is very important (see Fig. 3-4). Most of the traffic entering and leaving a bedroom is to or from a bathroom, and guests should have some degree of privacy when traveling to the bathroom. For the sake of comfort and convenience, it only makes sense to have the bathrooms near the bedrooms. Locating bathrooms in a particular area of the house is not as easy as positioning other rooms, specifically for remodeling jobs. Baths must have access to hot and cold water lines as well as drains and electrical wiring. It can be an awkward, and sometimes expensive, endeavor to tie into existing utilities when they are on the other end of the house.

Service Areas

Service areas include rooms like kitchens, laundry rooms, and garages. As you will see later, home shoppers regard the kitchen as one of the most important rooms in the house, at least when comparing one house to another. Buyers will often choose one house simply on the basis of the kitchen. The shining, colorful appliances and fixtures that make up a kitchen provide you with a real opportunity to show off your house.

It's not surprising that kitchens are one of the most expensive rooms in the house to design and build, (Fig. 3-6). There are a number of functions (food preparation, cooking, cleaning, and storage) that require specialized and expensive fixtures, appliances, and cabinets, all of which must be accounted for in the design and layout stage.

One reason the kitchen is so important to home shoppers is that it is the most central room in the house, at least in terms of family life. Family members tend to meet in the kitchen at meal times. Having an attractive, efficient kitchen helps make that experience a pleasant one.

In most families, grocery shopping takes place once or twice a week. There are few tasks around the household that are more arduous than hauling grocery bags, particularly when the sacks are split or torn, all the way through the house just to reach the kitchen. Consequently, it might be convenient to have easy access to the kitchen from the garage or driveway (Fig. 3-7). At the same time, you might want to locate the kitchen near a dining room, if the house has one, so that food, dishes, and utensils can be easily carried back and forth. Finally, access to a family room or patio might be a plus for many buyers. What all this means is that a centrally located kitchen is very important to a large number of families.

Once the location of the kitchen has been decided, consider the floor plan of the room itself. You need adequate storage and cupboard space as well as sufficient countertops and working space. If meals are to be served in the kitchen, allocate space for tables and chairs or counters and stools. Part of the problem with laying out a kitchen is that plans must be completed very early in the design stage. Once decided, plans often become ironclad because the kitchen has extensive electrical and plumbing requirements. It is plainly more difficult to move a sink or counter from one side of the room to another in the kitchen than it is to move a bed to another side of the room in the bedroom.

Other rooms that are usually considered part of the service area are utility rooms, laundry rooms (see Fig. 3-4), garages, basements, and attics. Except for the laundry room and sometimes the garage, these areas typically do not have specialized functions, and oftentimes, the rooms

Fig. 3-6. *Typical kitchen (courtesy of Merillat Industries, Inc.).*

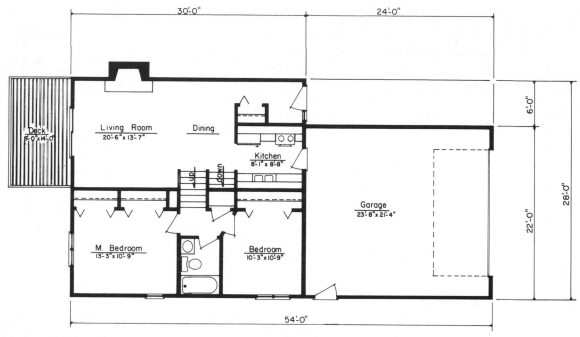

Fig. 3-7. *This floor plan provides easy access to the kitchen from the car in the garage, making it easier to carry groceries (courtesy of Fleetwood Homes, Inc.).*

are combined. You might find the laundry and utility facilities behind a single door, or the laundry might be located in the garage or basement.

Just as with kitchens, you must decide early in the design stage as to where you will locate service facilities. A clothes dryer installed in a garage, for instance, needs either 220-volt electrical wiring or gas lines as well as a vent to the outside of the house. In most cases, it is less expensive and more convenient if the service areas are located against outside walls and near the kitchen or baths so that utilities can be run with maximum efficiency.

Storage areas usually don't require any special utility needs other than lighting. Shelving, clothes hanging bars, and special storage compartments for large record or book collections might require extra bracing at the subfloor level. Care must be taken not to overload the attic with weight. You need adequate walkways so that you don't find yourself accidentally stepping through the living room ceiling. Although basements can provide more than enough space, they are usually too damp for some storage requirements unless special equipment, such as sump pumps and dehumidifiers are installed.

HOUSEHOLD TRAFFIC PATTERNS

Key to the effectiveness of any floor plan is the efficient and convenient channeling of household traffic. You probably don't want

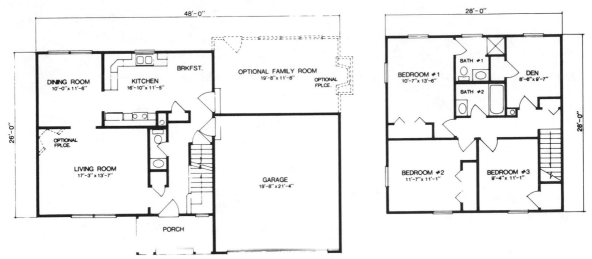

Fig. 3-8. *This floor plan has a convenient front entry hall and easy access to the kitchen from either the front door or the garage (courtesy of Fleetwood Homes, Inc.).*

children to come through a single entrance to the house if that entrance means they must walk through a formal, carpeted living room when it is wet and muddy outside. Neither is it desirable for guests to pass through the kitchen or other group room when they are traveling from their bedroom to the bath to take a shower. In general, treat rooms as a terminus to traffic, not an artery. When you are sitting in a room, you shouldn't have to watch people walking by. If traffic must pass through a room, try to channel it so that it flows through a corner or to one side, not across the center of the room.

When defining household traffic, you must consider two primary patterns: *indoor/outdoor traffic* and *room-to-room traffic.*

The primary indoor/outdoor entry is usually the front door. If at all possible, it should provide a direct path to a group area without passing through any personal or private rooms. This implies some sort of entry or hallway, particularly in those parts of the country where inclement weather is common.

Both you and your guests will appreciate a place to remove wet footgear or heavy coats. *Mudrooms* located at side or rear entrances might also be appropriate in certain regions. Make other indoor/outdoor entries convenient for kitchen access and removal of trash. Figure 3-8 illustrates a floor plan that provides a front entryway as well as easy access to the kitchen from the garage.

Remodeled houses in particular often have inefficient traffic patterns. The only passage to a patio, for instance, might be through a bedroom, or garages might open into living rooms. If at all possible, avoid such awkward traffic situations. The traffic resulting from a converted garage like the one in Fig. 3-9 can cause more problems than it solves.

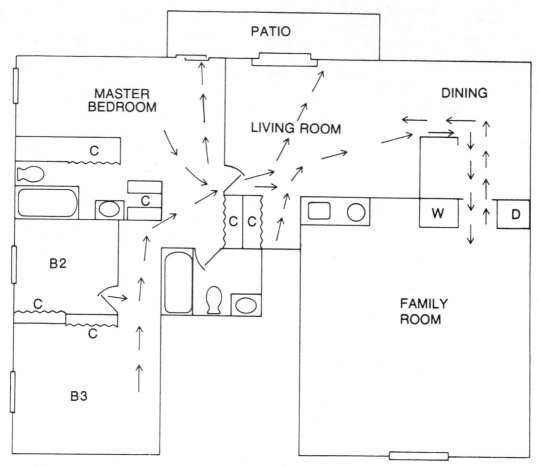

Fig. 3-9. *Remodeled houses sometimes produce inefficient traffic patterns.*

Inside the house, it is important that the different zones of the house be separated. It would be inconvenient to have a service room like the garage or the laundry room next to a bedroom. Obviously, a car pulling into a garage late at night makes enough noise to awake someone sleeping in an adjoining room. With multilevel homes, ground-floor level garages are often directly below bedrooms. Unless adequate sound barriers and insulation are provided, the noise might be just as bad as if the garage were on the other side of an interior wall.

Overlap between zones is sometimes necessary, even desirable. It is often handy, for instance, to have a personal room like a half-bath near a group room like a family or living room. Because many homeowners either plan on or end up using one of the bedrooms as a home office, it might also be a good idea to locate a bedroom near the service or living areas instead of the personal zones as well as locating it near a half-bath. If business associates will be entering the house for meetings in such rooms, it might also be advantageous to have an indoor/outdoor entry near the room. Avoid traffic problems on the top floor of two-story houses by keeping the stairs centrally situated so that a weblike layout of hallways isn't necessary.

If any room in the house should be considered central, that room is the kitchen. Lay it out to provide easy access to the dining room, to be near an indoor/outdoor entry (preferably one with access to the garage or driveway), and to be near a bathroom. Even though the kitchen might be the focal point of family life and has a couple of doors into the room, it doesn't necessarily have to be squarely in the center of the house, requiring family members to walk through the kitchen when going from the living room to the bedrooms.

Lay out rooms like the living room, that are used for entertaining guests to discourage through traffic. One way to ensure this is to situate the room so that it has only one entrance. You might want a secondary door, allowing entry into the dining room. The dining room can then have another door, allowing access to the kitchen.

Because storage and utility areas are sometimes dealt with as afterthoughts, they can pose unique problems. Laundry areas, for instance, can have a number of conflicting requirements. You might want the laundry area near the kitchen so that you can do simultaneous housework and so that it can share plumbing lines. On the other hand, having the laundry facilities near bedrooms or main bathrooms can save carrying linens and clothes from one end of the house to the other. If it is important to have the laundry in the personal zones of the house, closet or stacked washers and dryers provide an attractive alternative.

Utility rooms usually harbor furnaces, water heaters, air-conditioning units, and sometimes the washer and dryer. If a utility room is desired in the house, keep it away from the sleeping and living areas. Furnaces make more than enough noise to disturb people sleeping in the bedrooms. Also, utility rooms and the machines in them sometimes require the attention of electricians or plumbers. You can avoid the traffic and clutter associated with repairs if the room is situated away from the main living area of the house. The floor plan shown in Fig. 3-10 locates a utility room that includes laundry appliances, furnace, and a powder room in the basement of the house.

THE OPEN-PLANNING ALTERNATIVE

Today's floor plans and designs place a greater emphasis on informality than did home designs of several decades ago. One way home designers have achieved this effect is by the construction of open, multipurpose rooms that allow the occupant to define the layout in an individual, free-form manner. This trend is referred to as *open planning*.

Open planning, in essence, eliminates the physical walls between rooms that have compatible functions—formal living rooms and formal

Fig. 3-10. *The utility room in this house is located in the basement, away from the mainstream of family life (courtesy of Fleetwood Homes, Inc.).*

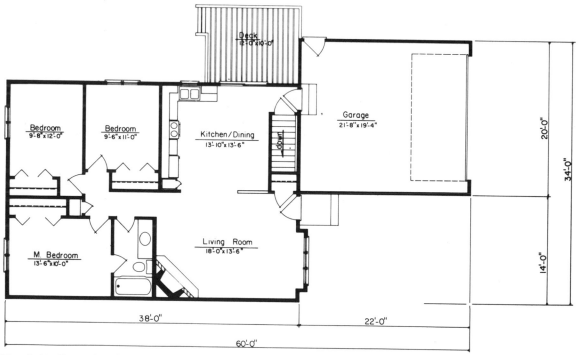

Fig. 3-11. *Open planning is the idea behind this floor plan (courtesy of Fleetwood Homes, Inc.).*

dining rooms, for example. Most of the living rooms and dining rooms illustrated in this chapter can coexist in a single area, as can kitchens and family rooms. Within the master suite, you might find a bedroom, a sitting room, an exercise room, and a bath. The floor plan in Fig. 3-11 illustrates a typical design of an *open* house. Notice that the living room, dining room, and kitchen essentially consist of a single room. Additionally, the sliding glass doors in the kitchen that lead to an outside deck add to the sense of openness.

The sense of spaciousness that open planning delivers also gives the impression that a room is larger than it actually is. In reality, open planning does add floor space to a house. A typical 8-foot long (linear) interior wall consumes about 4 square feet of floor space. By eliminating 40 linear feet of interior walls, designers can add about 20 square feet of living space to a house. In many instances, advances in structural materials have developed stronger, lighter building materials that make it possible to build open-space homes with greater distances between load-bearing walls.

EVALUATING FLOOR PLANS

So how do you go about evaluating the *traffic effectiveness* of a particular floor plan? First of all, scrutinize how the layout moves traffic through the house. If the kitchen and family room are the focal points of the house, what rooms do you have to walk through to get to them? If someone needs to go outside, will they have to pass through the kitchen? Is it possible for someone to take a shower and return to their bedroom without having to go through a group activity area? Are you able to take the shortest possible path when carrying groceries from the car to the kitchen?

When you are sure that the traffic patterns meet your and other people's requirements, consider the amount of privacy the floor plan extends. Is there someplace for you or others to get away? Is room available for quiet-time activities like reading or letter writing? Is there space available for messy chores like furniture refinishing? What about noisy activities like musical practice? Keep in mind that more than 80 percent of today's home buyers indicate that they will be spending more time at home. Does a house plan provide adequate space for home entertainment activities?

Ultimately, you might need to add on to the structure. There are house plans that lend themselves to future expansions. Most often, bedrooms, bathrooms, and family rooms are added as families grow. You can also plan for future enlargement by weighing plumbing and electrical layouts and house placement on the building site. Doing so will make the remodeling job much easier for you or future owners. Buyers will often settle for a house that is smaller than their actual or expected needs if the price is right and if the addition can be completed economically.

HOME DESIGNS

The design of a house is, as a rule, prescribed by the particular architectural style picked by the homeowner or builder. There are a number of common house styles—*ranch* (Fig. 3-12), *southern colonial* (Fig. 3-13), *French provincial* (Fig. 3-14), *English Tudor* (Fig. 3-15), *contemporary* (Fig. 3-16), and so on—that have, over the years, consistently appealed

Fig. 3-12. Ranch-style house (courtesy of New England Homes, Inc.).

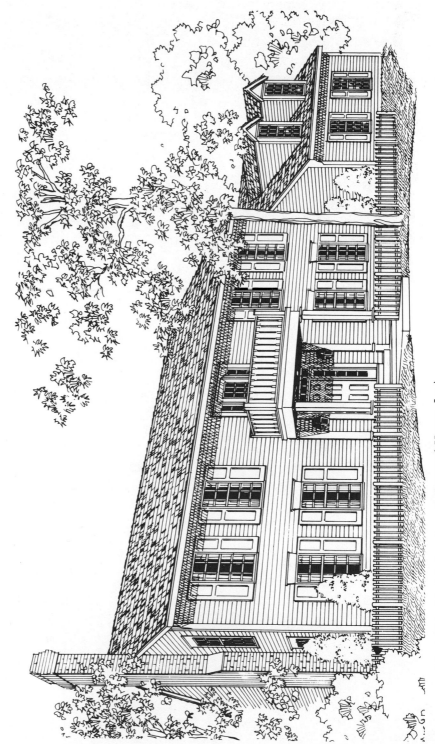

Fig. 3-13. Southern Colonial style (courtesy of Fleetwood Homes, Inc.).

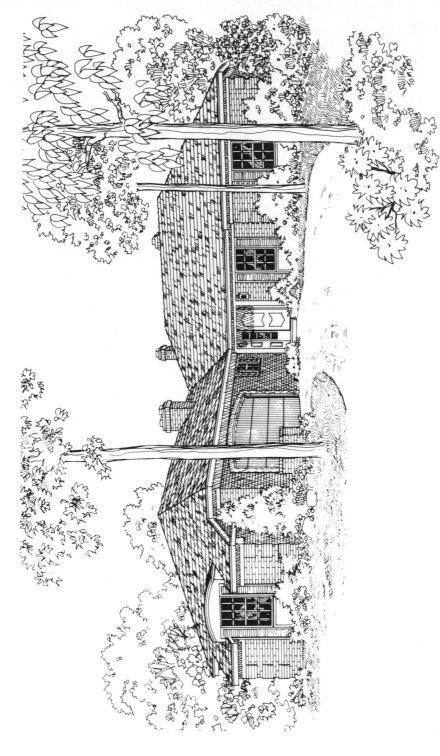

Fig. 3-14. *French Provincial style (courtesy of Fleetwood Homes, Inc.).*

Fig. 3-15. English Tudor style (courtesy of Fleetwood Homes, Inc.).

Fig. 3-16. Contemporary style (courtesy of Fleetwood Homes, Inc.).

to a wide range of home shoppers. If you are truly concerned about the resale value of the house you are buying or building, you would be well-advised to select a house that falls within the mainstream of architectural styles.

What eventually determines the style of your house is your own particular preferences and tastes. There are, however, a number of other factors that will influence your selection. One prime factor is the neighborhood in which your house will be built. If all of the houses on the street are single-story, ranch or contemporary homes, for instance, you shouldn't build a three-story southern colonial mansion no matter how badly you want that kind of house. You would be ahead to find a neighborhood where the house would not seem so out of place. (You might try to determine what it is you like about that style, however, then with the help of an architect, try to incorporate those features into a more appropriate style.)

Some house styles are more popular in certain parts of the country than other styles. Ranch or contemporary styles that are favored in Southern California are less popular in the northeast part of the country. Conversely, New England tends to have more *Cape Cod saltboxes* (like that in Fig. 3-17) than Arizona. Contemporary houses are preferred by about one-third of all home shoppers, while only about 15 percent want colonial styles. True Victorian, Spanish, and English Tudor homes, however, are each only favored by nearly 5 percent of the buyers.

While tradition is part of the reason buyers tend to favor conventional styles, geography plays a role too. One reason houses in the northeastern states have historically had steep roofs is to prevent excess weight build up from heavy snowfalls. Because snowfall isn't a problem in the southwest, houses there usually have flatter roofs.

Other factors that influence the style used to build a house include money and size. Some styles inherently cost more to build than others. A simple, boxlike house costs less to build than one that has a complicated outside wall structure and a complex roofline. Houses built in a southern colonial style are often larger than other types of houses, and they consequently require larger building lots. If you have a small lot and all of the other houses on the block are built to scale, then you will probably be making a mistake if you build a large, grandiose house.

Once you have selected a style of house that meets your general requirements, you need to decide whether or not that style is consistent with other selection criteria you might have. You should ask yourself what type of house you want. Do you want a single-story, a split-level, or a multifloor house?

Split-level and Multilevel Designs

Split-level or multifloor houses provide maximum privacy and unique decorating opportunities. *Split-level* homes (see Fig. 3-18) can easily be

Fig. 3-17. *Cape Cod style (courtesy of New England Homes, Inc.).*

Fig. 3-18. Split-level home (courtesy of New England Homes, Inc.).

41

designed to be built on sloping, hillside lots, enabling homeowners to take full advantage of scenic views. Split-level homes are preferred by about one out of four or five home shoppers.

Multilevel homes are usually laid out according to different living zones. As Fig. 3-19 shows, bedrooms tend to be on one level; living rooms, dining rooms, and kitchens on another; and service and utility rooms on yet another level. One-and-a-half story homes are the least popular multistory homes, appealing to less than 10 percent of all home shoppers. Two-story houses fare much better with almost one out of every three shoppers saying that they would prefer this type.

From a selling point of view, it might be difficult to sell a split-level (or multilevel) house to retirees or to shoppers who must care for elderly or handicapped family members who might have problems negotiating the stairs. Figure 3-20 shows a *single-floor* home that was designed primarily for such shoppers. Almost three out of every four retirees suggest that they prefer single-floor homes.

Single-floor Designs

When compared to multilevel homes, single-story homes have both advantages and disadvantages. On one hand, single-story homes, which are preferred by between 40 and 45 percent of today's home shoppers, are easier to get around in and, consequently, easier to clean and otherwise maintain. On the other hand, they tend to provide less privacy. Single-story houses also impart a greater sense of informality than do multistory houses. This can be the plus you want, but a definite minus if you are trying to achieve a more formal ambiance. It is more difficult to regulate and control traffic patterns in single-story homes than in multifloor structures.

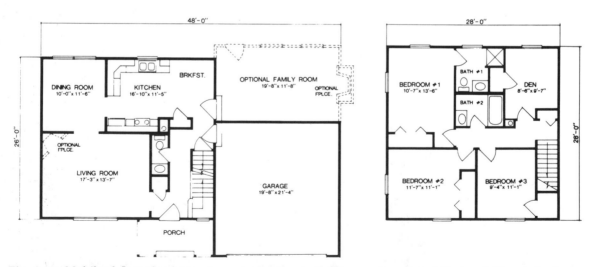

Fig. 3-19. *Multilevel floor plan lays out rooms according to living zones (courtesy of Fleetwood Homes, Inc.).*

Eclectic Designs

Eclectic or otherwise nonstandard home designs (like those homes shown at the beginning of Chapter 2) are also fine. By opting for such a design, however, you are probably minimizing rather than maximizing the resale value of your house because the house will appeal to a somewhat more limited number of potential buyers.

Contemporary Designs

Special consideration should be given to *contemporary* home designs because, over the past few decades, they have appealed to the widest

Fig. 3-20. *Single-level home designed with retirees in mind (courtesy of New England Homes, Inc.).*

available range of home shoppers. In fact, nearly one out of every three home shoppers have indicated they prefer contemporary designs. Furthermore, there is every indication that this trend will continue for the coming decades.

What do contemporary homes offer that attract so many buyers? For one thing, contemporary homes are designed to accent open space and provide access to the outdoors. There is little question that people today spend more of their time and resources on outdoor recreational activities than ever before. To provide this access, today's contemporary homes tend to have large windows and doors that open onto the outdoor living areas of the house, typically the backyard (which provides more privacy) instead of the front.

Contemporary home designs also usually require less maintenance and upkeep than other house styles, again consistent with the desire for recreational-oriented life-styles. Accordingly, many contemporary homes are built from low-maintenance brick or stone. (About 50 percent of all home shoppers say they prefer houses that have brick or masonry siding.) They are built along horizontal lines that are not as difficult to maintain as the vertically-oriented homes of previous generations. The sometimes large expanse of windows cuts down on major maintenance, like house painting, as well.

Many people mistakenly equate the term *contemporary* with *modernistic*. Homes built along strict boxlike, high-tech, modernistic lines appeal to a limited number of people, however, and shoppers are often turned off just by hearing that a particular home is "contemporary." For whatever reasons, home shoppers prefer houses that are more traditional in style. In fact, 72 percent of home buyers interviewed in a Lou Harris poll said that they preferred an upscale version of the traditionally designed homes in which they grew up in back in the 1950s.

Instead of designing houses that are either completely modern or traditional, what architects and builders have done is create houses around hybrid designs. A house that is primarily contemporary, for instance, might have a slight traditional flavor. The house in Fig. 3-21, for example, is a contemporary house with Victorian design features. As most of the houses shown in this chapter illustrate, contemporary homes can be adapted to virtually any traditional design, from Cape Cod to California ranchero.

BUYER PREFERENCE

With all of the possible design options, it is sometimes difficult to decide which floor plans or which house styles to base your plans around. Factors such as geography, climate, and even local zoning restrictions can influence the overall design of a particular house. Nonetheless, home

Fig. 3-21. *Contemporary home designed along Victorian lines (courtesy of Fleetwood Homes, Inc.).*

shoppers have expressed preferences in terms of design and layout, preferences that they are willing to pay for.

For the most part, home shoppers have indicated that they like a multistory house based on a contemporary, open layout, such as the roughly 1900 square foot design shown in Fig. 3-22. The favored layout concentrates group activities onto the first or ground floor, while setting aside the second floor for personal living areas.

The house that appeals to the widest range of home shoppers should have four bedrooms, three of which are located on the second floor, with the fourth on the ground floor. About one-third of shoppers indicate they want the guest bedroom on the ground floor. Slightly more shoppers, however, indicate that they want all of the bedrooms on the second floor. The ground-floor bedroom would double as a home office or den and would be near both an outside entryway and a half-bath. For those buyers who must care for an elderly or handicapped person who might have problems climbing stairs, having a downstairs bedroom and bath is even more important.

The front entrance of the house, say home shoppers, should not open into any specific room but into a hall or entryway. The primary traffic pattern of the front door should lead into an informal room such as the family room. Someone should not have to walk through the family room on the way to another group living area. It should have direct access to

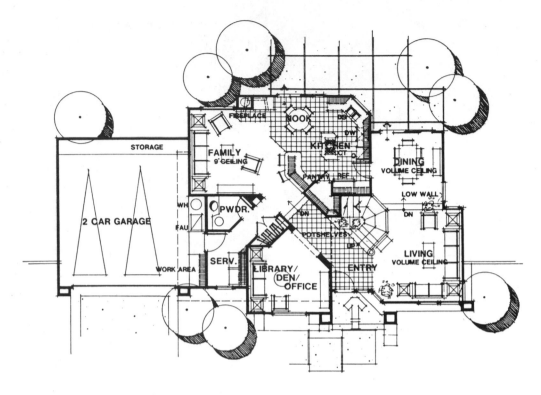

FIRST FLOOR

FRONT ELEVATION

Fig. 3-22. *Typical floor plan designed around home shopper's stated preferences (courtesy of The Smets Architectural Group, Inc.).*

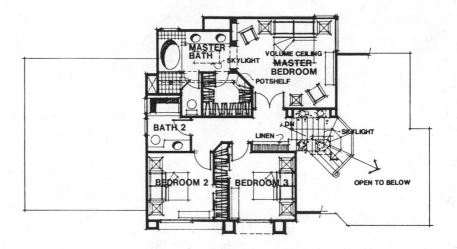

SECOND FLOOR

Fig. 3-22. *(Continued from page 46.)*

formal areas such as the living and dining room. Visitors coming to the house for a formal occasion should not have to walk through an informal family room to visit or dine. About 80 percent of home shoppers indicate that the formal living room should be in the front of the house, while a slightly lower number want the dining room in the rear. When it comes to trade-offs in room size, most home shoppers would rather have a larger family room and smaller dining room than the inverse. Notice that the sample floor plan has a fireplace in the family room instead of the living room; again, this is consistent with buyer preferences.

Buyers have suggested that they want the kitchen to be in a location that is central to both informal living and formal dining areas. Because more traffic and activity will be between the kitchen and family room instead of the kitchen and dining room, the kitchen should open on the living area. The kitchen should also provide an informal dining area of its own, again which opens on the family room.

Because so much of today's family activities are both privacy and outdoor-oriented, the family room and the kitchen should provide convenient and safe access to the backyard. This will allow small children to go back and forth between the family room and kitchen or family room and backyard, yet still allow adults to easily supervise the children's actions. Well over half of home buyers say they like a rear-facing kitchen and family room layout.

As in the sample layout, moderately direct access to the kitchen from a two-car garage is preferred by over half of the buyers. It can house the furnace, hot-water heater, storage, and work areas. Laundry facilities should be separate from the other work areas, yet still close at hand. Buyers prefer not to have the washer and dryer in the garage. Still, the household won't be thrown into disarray if plumbing or other problems requiring repair is necessary. It is no surprise, then, that nearly three out of four home shoppers say they prefer the laundry in a room next to the garage.

The second floor of the house is devoted to personal living areas dominated by a large master suite. A large walk-in closet with plenty of storage space is of prime importance to home shoppers. Even though the sample floor plan has a dressing or sitting area, it is important that the closets are relatively large. Four out of five home shoppers have indicated that they would prefer to have walk-in closets and a smaller dressing or sitting area as opposed to one out of four who prefer the opposite. The master suite should face the rear of the house. This is very important to buyers because the rear of the house is more private and less bothered by excess noise than those rooms on the front of the house. Three out of four home shoppers, in fact, have indicated that they prefer the master suite in the rear.

The other bedrooms have slider-door closets and easy, and somewhat private, access to a bathroom that is separate from the master suite's. When designing a secondary bath, note that a majority of shoppers have indicated they prefer a separate tub and shower arrangement over a single shower stall or a shower/tub combination.

4

Kitchens and Service Areas

OVER THE YEARS, THE KITCHEN HAS REMAINED THE CROSS-road of the home. It is the room where family members convene, converse, and generally keep in touch. And, when it comes to selling your home, it is the room that is probably more important than any other. Home shoppers overwhelming have said that the design and location of the kitchen is a crucial part—perhaps the *most* crucial part—of their buying decision. This isn't surprising because the typical homeowner spends more waking hours in the kitchen than in any other room in the house. If this leads you to assume that buyers want larger food preparation areas with eating areas nearby, then you are beginning to get a picture of what home shoppers are looking for.

The kitchen is often regarded as a service area of the house because much of the activity in the kitchen is aimed at providing services, such as food preparation, for the entire family. (Other household services include laundry, heating, and so on.) Consequently, the general floor plan of a house might locate the kitchen near other service-oriented areas like the laundry or utility room.

KITCHENS

Showcasing the kitchen is an easy way of attracting buyers' attention. The room provides you with the best available opportunity to show off bright colors, shiny surfaces, and innovative, but homey, designs.

In terms of building materials and utility requirements, the kitchen is considered the most complex room in the house, even more so than the bathroom. It includes both hot and cold water; drains for everything from dishwashers to ice makers; special wiring for appliances such as garbage disposals and microwaves; and natural gas lines for stoves, grills, and ovens. The kitchen also has special surfacing requirements ranging from flooring, to countertops, to cabinets, and food serving areas. Every family member, from grandparents to toddlers, has access to the room, and it must be designed to accommodate all of their needs.

When planning or evaluating a kitchen, you must consider the activities that take place in it. The kitchen is probably the only room in the house where food is actually prepared. The room might be one of two or three eating areas, however, and space must be set aside for food consumption. For both of these reasons, the kitchen is a key room when you are entertaining guests. To accommodate these various activities, the kitchen needs adequate working space—counter space, moving around space, and storage space.

You also must know the various appliances that are used in kitchens. You might consider some appliances indispensable, while others might be optional. Future owners of the house might have different priorities, so if you are building a house or remodeling a kitchen, you might want to include wiring or plumbing to make it easier for potential buyers to install other appliances.

LAYOUT STRATEGIES

Even though one kitchen is different from every other kitchen, there are really only about a half-dozen basic kitchen layouts. Variations on those basic floor plans provide many alternatives, but many kitchens are essentially the same. Those basic floor plans include a single-counter kitchen, two-counter kitchen, L-shaped kitchen, U-shaped kitchen, and island kitchen.

As the list suggests, the arrangement of counters defines the basic kitchen floor plan in the room. The arrangement significantly affects the traffic and work patterns that you and others follow when working in or passing through the kitchen.

The Work Triangle

Most of the work that gets done in any kitchen involves the sink, stove, and refrigerator. As Fig. 4-1 illustrates, the typical person accomplishes most kitchen-related tasks by traveling to and from these three work areas, called the *work triangle*. If any one of the three is

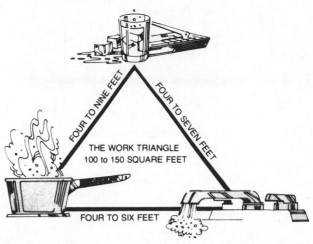

Fig. 4-1. *Most work in the kitchen is accomplished in a triangular pattern (courtesy of Merillat Industries, Inc.).*

separated from the other two, the work pattern is very inefficient. Some homeowners try to get by with locating a refrigerator in another room, perhaps a pantry or dining room, but such an arrangement is highly undesirable.

For maximum efficiency, make the sink/stove/refrigerator no less than 4 feet from each other and no more than about 7 or 8 feet. Looking at it another way, the sum of the three sides of the resulting work triangle should total no less than 12 feet or more than 22 or 23 feet. Because most people end up traveling between the stove and sink more than the other possible combinations, you might want that distance to be slightly less.

Home buyers will not go into a kitchen looking for an efficient work triangle. If a kitchen has an inefficient layout, however, you can bet they will notice. Effort spent on enhancing a kitchen that is inefficient in the first place will go, where else? down the drain.

Because so much family life takes place in the kitchen, many buyers might find a room with a greater than usual amount of floor space very attractive. In such cases, it might be impossible to have a relatively compact triangle, but you might lay out the floor plan to implement more than one work triangle, particularly if the kitchen includes an island.

Traffic Patterns

Chapter 3 discussed how traffic patterns can affect the overall layout and design of a house. The kitchen presents a unique problem in that it probably generates more traffic and has more potential dangers than any other room in the house. During the design and evaluation phase, careful thought must be given to how people move through the room. You don't want a floor plan that encourages children to run through the kitchen on their way outside, possibly bumping into hot stoves or

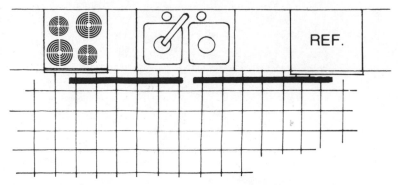

Fig. 4-2. *Single-counter kitchen floor plan and work pattern (courtesy of Merillat Industries, Inc.).*

knocking over foodstuffs. A safe design should provide a pathway that is between 3 and 4 feet wide.

What influences kitchen traffic patterns more than anything else is the location of doors that lead into and out of the room. If you want to control traffic, you must first control placement of the doors. There's usually nothing wrong with having people pass through the kitchen, as long as they don't trespass from traffic areas into work areas.

In some island kitchens, for instance, the shortest distance between two doors directs traffic on the side of the island that is between the sink and island stove top. This is inefficient and dangerous. In this case, it would be better to design the kitchen so that access to the door causes people to walk on the opposite side of the island.

Single-Counter Kitchen Floor Plans

Single-counter kitchens, sometimes called *galley* or *corridor kitchens*, are most often implemented in limited-space areas. Figure 4-2 shows a typical single-counter floor plan.

Single-counter kitchens are somewhat deceiving. On one hand, they appear to make efficient use of available space. On the other hand, they provide the most inefficient work space of all possible designs because the distances of traffic and work patterns are much greater. Consequently, people tend to build single-counter kitchens when houses, cabins, apartments, or vacation cottages are cramped for space.

For maximum possible efficiency, the total length of such a kitchen should be about 20 feet. Locate the sink in a single-counter kitchen near the center of the counter.

Two-Counter Kitchen Floor Plans

As Fig. 4-3 illustrates, the only real difference between a single-counter kitchen and a *two-counter kitchen* is that appliances and work areas are parallel to each other instead of linear. One counter typically consists of

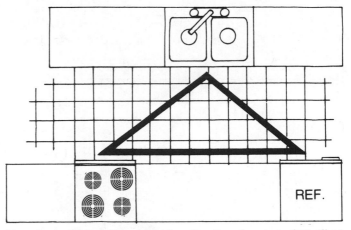

Fig. 4-3. *Two-counter kitchen floor plan and work pattern (courtesy of Merillat Industries, Inc.).*

a counter with a centrally located sink. The other work area is primarily made up of a refrigerator and stove.

Ideally, the opposing work areas in a two-counter, also called a *pullman*, kitchen should be no more than about 4½ feet apart. This floor plan is very efficient and found in many houses. If doorways are located at both ends of the kitchen, however, the kitchen can attract a lot of traffic. This makes it difficult to get work done in what is essentially a small working area.

L-Shaped Kitchen Floor Plans

The L-*shaped kitchen layout*, like that shown in Fig. 4-4, is perhaps the most popular kitchen layout because it provides an efficient, flexible, and attractive floor plan. As with most kitchens, this layout has a central sink with a stove and refrigerator on both legs of the L.

The corner formed by the intersection of the two perpendicular counters creates a large and attractive work area. In some kitchens, one counter can be used as a room divider or serving/breakfast bar.

U-Shaped Kitchen Floor Plans

For those homes that have enough available space, many home builders are turning to U-*shaped kitchens*, Fig. 4-5. In this layout, three counters are connected with the sink typically positioned at the base of the U. The stove and refrigerator can then be divided between the two other counters or built into a single side with a room divider/breakfast bar on the opposing counter. U-shaped layouts do not allow through traffic because one end of the room is obviously a dead end. This can mean that as people congregate in the kitchen, it can become very crowded because there is no real way for traffic to flow.

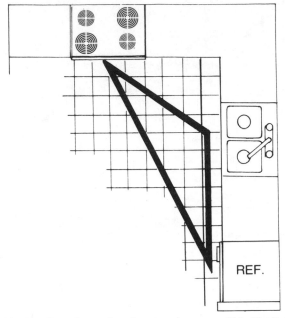

Fig. 4-4. *L-shaped kitchen floor plan and work pattern (courtesy of Merillat Industries, Inc.).*

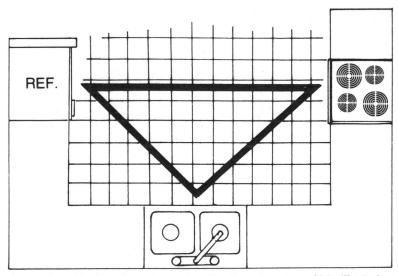

Fig. 4-5. *U-shaped kitchen floor plan and work pattern (courtesy of Merillat Industries, Inc.).*

Part of the reason people like a U-shaped kitchen is because they are efficient and compact. This can work against you, however, if the room isn't square enough to provide ample working space or if there simply isn't enough room. Allow for at least 8 or 9 feet from wall-to-wall across the U. Cabinets that are uniquely fitted to a specific space might also be required, and such cabinets are often expensive.

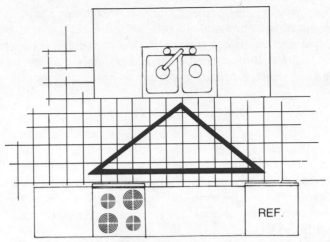

Fig. 4-6. *Island kitchen floor plan and work pattern (courtesy of Merillat Industries, Inc.).*

Island Kitchen Floor Plans

Island work areas provide kitchens with some of the most flexible floor plans possible. As long as there is enough room, islands can be adapted to fit in just about any of the other kitchen floor plans, particularly U-shaped and L-shaped. A typical island kitchen floor plan is shown in Fig. 4-6.

Free-standing islands can be put to just about any use required by kitchen activities. This includes food preparation (Fig. 4-7), cooking, and washing. Often, food preparation islands are set on casters and can be moved around the kitchen as needed. Islands like this are not only handy, but they enable you to easily redecorate an area. Islands that are built for cooking or otherwise have utilities (gas, water, or electricity) attached to them cannot be moved. These islands need adequate room for people to comfortably and safely walk around them. The combined measurements of the island and the open space on both sides of the unit should not be less than 10 feet.

Evaluating Kitchen Layouts

The effectiveness of a specific floor plan depends upon a number of factors. Some of these factors involve intangibles, such as work patterns and traffic patterns, while other factors include safety and location of appliances and utilities. Kitchens are also unique in that their floor plans extend beyond or, more appropriately, above the floor itself, especially when you consider the importance of wall-mounted cabinets.

When evaluating kitchen layouts, keep in mind that there are several standard tasks that are usually done in the kitchen and that space for each must be accounted for. Tasks that require space include food preparation (cutting block, access to a garbage disposal), food storage (refrigerator, freezer, and pantry), cooking areas (stove top, oven, and microwave), utensil storage (cabinets and drawers), sink areas (for washing food and utensils), and eating. A haphazard arrangement of these areas will result in an inefficient and possibly dangerous kitchen, something that is often readily apparent to home shoppers.

DESIGN STRATEGIES

When it comes to attractive designs, few rooms in a house offer the possibilities that the kitchen offers simply because there are so many alternatives. Between all of the options for cabinets, appliances, flooring, and countertops, the variety seems almost infinite. You should do whatever you can to take advantage of these options because the kitchen provides you with a rare opportunity to really show off your house to prospective buyers.

Attractive, efficient kitchens aren't cheap. In fact, if you are remodeling the kitchen, you can end up spending more money on it than

Fig. 4-7. *Kitchen with a free-standing storage/preparation island (courtesy of Merillat Industries, Inc.).*

any other room in the house. A typical kitchen remodeling project, which includes new cabinets, new stove top, and so on, can cost more than $10,000. Because kitchens are so important to buyers, however, you shouldn't have any problems recovering almost all of this money when you sell the house. Most home shoppers recognize the expense required to remodel a kitchen too. If they see an outdated or inefficient kitchen that obviously needs remodeling, buyers might lose interest in the house or not be willing to pay your asking price.

The design and style of the kitchen should mirror that of the interior of the house as a whole. If you have established a country motif throughout the house, follow it through in the kitchen. If, on the other hand, the house is modern or contemporary in design, a country kitchen will unquestionably look out of place.

Kitchen Cabinets

Kitchen cabinets serve both a functional and aesthetic role. From a practical point of view, cabinets provide most of the storage required in the kitchen and support for countertops, sinks, stove tops, and other kitchen-related work areas. Kitchen cabinets also do more than anything else, however, to establish the tone or the atmosphere you want the kitchen to project. Cabinets can dominate the kitchen, if that's what you want. But if you want to focus attention on other design elements, the cabinets can simply provide a backdrop.

Whatever effect you are striving for, cabinets can be the most expensive elements in the kitchen. The one thing that buyers want in cabinets is quantity—the more cabinets, the better. It is doubtful that you can ever have enough cabinets in the kitchen.

Rooms that are odd-sized or have irregular corners will probably require custom cabinets that either can be built at a factory following precise measurements or built on the site. Rooms that are more conventional in size and shape can use prefab cabinets that fit into standard-size spaces.

As Fig. 4-8 illustrates, there are several different types of kitchen cabinets. *Base cabinets* rest on the floor and usually support countertops and other work areas. They are usually about 2 feet deep and 3 feet high. (Actually, the cabinet itself is usually only 34½ inches high with a 1½-inch countertop, bringing the total height to 36 inches.) A slight variation in the height of base cabinets, even an inch or two, can make a big difference for many people. Unusually low or high base cabinets will make the kitchen unacceptable to many buyers who will immediately realize they will have to tear out existing cabinets to bring them to a more appropriate height. Ensure that the base cabinet height is as close as possible to 36 inches.

Wall cabinets, on the other hand, are usually about 12 inches deep. Their height varies, depending on the height of the ceiling and how close

MATCHING WALL ANGLE CABINET •   • WALL CABINET

LAZY SUSAN
BASE CABINET •

• OVEN
CABINET

• BASE CABINET

UTILITY BASE CABINET •

Fig. 4-8. *Common types of kitchen cabinets (courtesy of Merillat Industries, Inc.).*

they are mounted to the countertop. Figure 4-9 illustrates the various dimensions. The height of wall cabinets is of less importance than with base cabinets.

Although the exterior finish of cabinets can consist of a variety of materials, wood and plastic laminate predominate. Wood-faced cabinets, like those in Fig. 4-10, have a broader appeal and, depending on the type of wood and the finish, is versatile enough to be used with just about any design. Plastic laminate cabinets (Fig. 4-11), however, tend to go better with more modern designs. The plastic laminate is strong and easy to clean.

Unless the underlying structure of the cabinets is well-built, high-quality, expensive exterior facing will be wasted. The structure should be solid, built of plywood or boards instead of particleboard, and the drawers should slide in and out on mechanical drawer guides and assemblies. The first thing knowledgeable home shoppers will do when

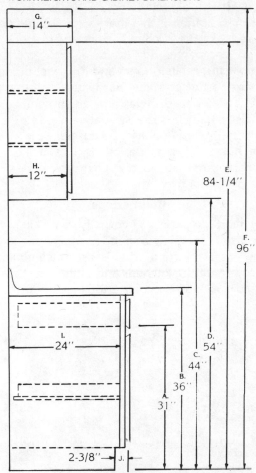

A. Counter height for planning
   area or sit-down area, 31" from
   floor.
B. Standard countertop, 36"
   from floor.
C. Wall switches and outlets, 44"
   from floor.
D. Bottom of 30" wall cabinet,
   54" from floor.
E. Top of wall cabinet, 84-1/4"
   from floor.
F. Ceiling, 96" from floor.
G. Depth of soffit, 14".
H. Depth of wall cabinet, 12" (not
   including doors).
I. Depth of base cabinet, 24"
   (not including doors).
J. Depth of toe space, 2-3/8".

Fig. 4-9. *Typical cabinet dimensions (courtesy of Merillat Industries, Inc.).*

inspecting a kitchen that has obviously new cabinets is open up the doors and examine the structural components.

One thing about cabinets is that there are a number of ways they can be spruced up to make the kitchen look more attractive to prospective buyers. There are companies, for example, that specialize in refacing cabinets or in replacing cabinet doors and drawers. Sometimes nothing more than a coat of paint and new hardware is all that's needed.

Built-in appliances like dishwashers, trash compactors, and even garbage disposals usually require special cabinetry. This needs to be planned for early in the design phase. Because these labor-saving devices are rated high on home shoppers' desirability lists, make sure the cabinets are designed to accommodate such appliances.

Countertops

The primary working surface in virtually every kitchen is the cabinet countertop. Because homeowners spend so much time looking at, working on, and cleaning it, the countertop is a surprisingly important factor when it comes to evaluating kitchens and ultimately houses. The choice of materials used for kitchen countertops varies from real wood to

Fig. 4-10. *Kitchen cabinets with wood exteriors (courtesy of Merillat Industries, Inc.).*

synthetic composites. Unlike some aspects of the kitchen, the countertop material itself isn't limited to any specific kitchen style. Variations of just about any material are available to be used with virtually every style.

Many countertops simply consist of particleboard covered with *plastic laminate*. Countertops such as these have certain advantages—they are generally less expensive than other materials, are usually easier to install, and usually can be cut-to-fit on the spot so you don't have to have exact measurements. Other materials, like stainless steel or marble, require exact and unforgiving measurements. Plastic laminate is also easy to clean and is available in a wide variety of patterns, including simulated wood, marble, brick, etc. On the negative side, the glue that adheres the laminate to the particleboard can become loose over time. Also, the laminate can become permanently stained from rusts or burns, and the surface, which isn't as hard as brick or ceramic tile, can become nicked and scratched by kitchen utensils and cutting tools.

Although plastic laminate countertops are probably more common than just about any other type, many home shoppers prefer *ceramic tile*.

Fig. 4-11. *Kitchen cabinets with plastic laminate exteriors (courtesy of Merillat Industries, Inc.).*

This countertop material is so popular because it is both very functional and very attractive to look at. It won't nick or scratch like wood or laminate, it is (or should be) water resistant, and it is easy to clean. Hot cooking utensils can be set on tile without damaging the surface.

Tiles are available in a wide variety of colors, patterns, and sizes. While ceramic tiles are more difficult to install than plastic laminate, it doesn't require as exact measurements as other types. If you are doing the tiling yourself, you can work around slight dimensional inaccuracies.

Even though *hardwoods* like oak or maple can make attractive countertops, they are not an ideal material unless the wood is properly finished to ensure that the material is waterproof. A couple of coats of polyurethane will provide a hard, waterproof surface, however, the wood will need to be refinished or treated every few years. Instead of using wood throughout the kitchen, you may find it best to limit wood countertops to areas that are used for eating, not washing.

Synthetic marble is one of the most durable of all kitchen countertop materials. It is waterproof, easy to clean, and strong. It comes in a variety of patterns and colors and is relatively easy to install, even for do-it-yourselfers. Synthetic marble, like *Corian* that is made by DuPont (Fig. 4-12), will not stain and scratch like real marble. If nicks do occur, they can be sanded and polished almost like wood.

Built-in Appliances

The basic appliances found in kitchens have traditionally been a stove and refrigerator. Today's home buyers expect a lot more from their kitchens than just the basics, however. For this reason, kitchens now have appliances that are more exotic and more complex than ever before.

To paraphrase Henry Ford, appliances used to come in any color you wanted—as long as that color was white. Today, appliances really do come in any color and pattern, including wood-grained and other exotic surfaces. Some appliance manufacturers even provide customization kits that let you add a unique finish to an appliance. This enables you to coordinate the refrigerator doors with wall coverings or cabinets. On the flip side, an appliance that has an out-of-fashion or dated color will look old and suggest to the home shopper that it might need repair in the near future. White is one of those colors that does not go out of style and is usually a safe bet for major appliances.

If you compare a *refrigerator* of today with a refrigerator of, say, 30 years ago, the first difference you will notice is that the walls of the older appliance are much thicker than that of the new unit. This is because the insulation of today's appliances is far superior to that of yesterday. All of today's appliances are also more energy efficient than ever before. This simply means that it takes less energy to power them today. Although home shoppers are generally less concerned about energy efficiency than home buyers of a few years ago, you are still ahead if you install energy-efficient appliances.

Refrigerators, for instance, now provide more storage space than older units while still taking up about the same floor space, usually about 2 feet deep and no more than 3 feet wide. The height, typically no more than 6 feet, is usually only an issue when a unit has to fit into a cabinet design. To a large degree, this additional storage is due to more efficient design and improved materials. Modern refrigerators usually provide about 20 cubic feet of storage space.

Because many homes have refrigerators that are specially selected for a particular kitchen, those refrigerators often remain with the house when it is sold. It is therefore important that when selecting a refrigerator, you choose one that appeals to a wide range of home shoppers. The features of a refrigerator that are important to buyers are, foremost, an *automatic defrosting system*. Some people stay away from self-defrosting refrigerators because they consume more energy than manual defrosting units. Over

Fig. 4-12. *Corian countertop. A synthetic marblelike material made by DuPont that is preferred by many home shoppers (courtesy of DuPont Co.).*

the past few years, however, home buyers have expressed a greater desire for convenience than for energy efficiency.

It is also important that the doors be hinged in the proper direction, that is, away from the nearest countertop. This makes it easier to move foodstuffs from the countertop into the refrigerator without having to walk around an open door. (Yes, refrigerators have left-hand and right-hand opening doors.) Side-by-side refrigerator/freezers can cause problems because a door will always be in the way no matter which part of the appliance you are opening.

Automatic ice makers and *external cold-water dispensers* are other popular features, even though they require that a waterline be connected to the refrigerator. Some buyers see these items as simply something more that can break down. If your refrigerator has optional features like this and they don't work, you will not encourage home shoppers to buy the house.

Equally important to home buyers is the *cooking equipment* that is used in the kitchen. This equipment can consist of a range, oven, microwave, grill, etc.

As with everything else in the kitchen, convenience is what is important to shoppers. This means not only convenience for cleaning, but also the convenience provided by the efficient location of appliances.

Free-standing ranges (with oven) have traditionally been the preferred cooking appliance. That preference is shifting, however, as homeowners turn to built-in surface cooktops with separate built-in ovens. Drop-in cooktops are often built into a cooking island that is centrally located in the kitchen. The cooking units usually have from two to six burners and might or might not have a grill. Typical cooktops are from 1 to 3 ½ feet in width and less than 2 feet deep. Size is important when a free-standing stove is to fit between two cabinets. If the cabinetmakers don't leave enough space, the stove won't fit into the slot, while leaving too much space creates an awkward working area. If the cooktop is built into the cabinet, height is not a problem; if a free-standing range is used, it should be very close to the same height as surrounding cabinets.

Built-in ovens are available in single or double units, usually stacked one on top of another (one oven for roasting and the other for broiling). Over the past few years, however, the second oven has been replaced by a *microwave oven*. The main thing about ovens is that they be self-cleaning. As with frost-free refrigerators, self-cleaning ovens consume more energy, but homeowners are willing to put up with marginally higher energy costs if it results in less drudgery. In any event, the microwave oven is an important appliance in today's kitchen, a big change from 10 years ago when microwaves were much more expensive and much less common.

Give some thought whether to use *electricity* or *gas* to energize the cooking equipment. If electricity is used, you need a 220/240-volt line. Many of today's home shoppers prefer gas, however. Island cooking stations, either electric or gas, also require special hookups. These islands are permanent and cannot be moved without first disconnecting and turning off the appropriate utility.

Automatic dishwashers have been in the kitchen longer than the microwave and are generally considered a standard kitchen appliance. Undercounter, built-in dishwashers are the preferred type. Locating the unit near the sink is both convenient and efficient—convenient because it makes work in the kitchen easier, and efficient in that the dishwasher is close to the existing water, drain, and electrical lines. The exact location of the dishwasher in the counter, whether in the center or at the end, isn't that important. What is important is that it be located near the sink and, most often, to the left of the sink because there are more right-handed than left-handed people.

Many dishwashers have exterior trim kits that enable you to closely match the appliance with the kitchen cabinets or with the other appliances in the room. This is an important cosmetic consideration because an appliance like the dishwasher can appear obtrusive and look out of place. When selecting a dishwasher, look for those that have above average insulation to keep noise to a minimum. No one likes a noisy appliance, and the dishwasher perhaps makes more noise than any other appliance in the kitchen.

Garbage disposals are another appliance that are now considered a necessity instead of a luxury by nearly three out of every four shoppers. When installed beneath the kitchen sink, some codes require a somewhat larger drain than normal. Additionally, disposals might require their own electrical circuit, particularly if they have a large motor (¾ hp or larger). Safety is an important consideration with a disposal. It is important to locate the switch where it is out of the reach of children and where it cannot be accidentally switched on while your hand is inside the unit dislodging or removing something.

Although the *kitchen sink* is not an electrical appliance, it is an important tool in the kitchen. Because a sink is used probably more than any other item in the kitchen, it is important that you choose a high-quality sink that you like. At one time, single-bowl, cast-iron, porcelain-coated sinks were the norm. Today's sinks are made from stainless steel, cast-iron, fiberglass, and synthetic materials. They are available with single-, double-, and even triple-bowls, and come in just about any color. Figure 4-13 shows a typical modern kitchen sink. Although stainless steel sinks are very popular, they do tend to vibrate more and make more noise when a garbage disposal is operating beneath them. Old sinks can easily be spruced up by simply replacing the faucet.

Floor Covering

Kitchen floors undergo more abuse than any other floor surface in the house. They have more things spilled on them and dropped on them than any other room, and they are, consequently, cleaned more. As the center of family life, kitchen floors also have more foot traffic than any other room. Because of all this, kitchen floor covering material must be durable. Carpets used in kitchens, for instance, are usually not the same carpets used in living rooms and bedrooms. Instead, kitchen carpets are totally synthetic with waterproof backing. In general, select flooring colors that are neutral and light.

The most commonly used floor covering material in kitchens is *resilient flooring*. Sometimes called *vinyl flooring*, resilient flooring like that in Fig. 4-14 comes in a variety of forms, from individual squares (9-×-9-inch square) to large sheets (6 to 12 feet wide). Pattern selections seem almost infinite, and vinyl flooring can come cushioned or uncushioned with wax or no-wax surfaces. Good resilient flooring has a relatively thick *clear wear*

Fig. 4-13. *A typical modern kitchen sink (courtesy of Kohler Co.).*

Fig. 4-14. *Inlaid vinyl floor covering is one type of resilient flooring (courtesy of Armstrong World Industries, Inc.).*

layer that is resistant to heat and other damages. You can assume that the thicker this layer, the better the floor covering. Avoid simulated patterns that replicate natural surfaces such as wood or stone because these can be perceived as cheap imitations.

Ceramic tile is an excellent material for covering kitchen floors. Although it is more expensive and more difficult to install than resilient flooring, it is more durable and more permanent. Ceramic tile that is used on the floor is not the same as tile used on countertops. You can usually get similar, if not matching, colors and patterns so that there is a sense of continuity between the two surface areas. Natural surface materials, like ceramic tile, quarry tile, and even wood, have become a preferred flooring material with many home shoppers.

One thing that is very important about ceramic tile floors is that they have an antiskid surface. Spilled water or grease can make kitchen floors very dangerous, particularly if the floor has a naturally slick surface like that of glazed ceramic tiles. Ceramic tiles also provide a cold surface and, when the tiles are used above an uninsulated ground floor in cold climates, can make the kitchen uncomfortable to be in.

Hardwood flooring can be used in the kitchen but, as with wood countertops, coat them with polyurethane so that the surface is both mar-resistant and waterproof. You can coordinate wooden floors with other floors in the house or with countertops and cabinets in the kitchen.

Wall and Ceiling Covering

With all of the attention that is paid to cabinets, countertops, and appliances in the kitchen, it is easy to gloss over the walls and ceiling. As with the floor, however, the walls and ceiling must withstand a lot more abuse than similar surfaces in other rooms of the house. Not only can there be more humidity in the kitchen than in other rooms, but cooking grease and fumes can cause problems if the room is not prepared for them.

If you choose to *paint* the walls and ceiling, you might want to use gloss or semigloss enamel because they can be more easily cleaned than flat paint. You might even consider using exterior acrylic house paint in the kitchen because exterior paint is tougher and will stand up better to cleaning than interior paint (leave the windows open during painting, however). Whenever possible, use neutral colors—whites or yellow pastels—for kitchen walls. Avoid covering large areas with dark colors. For whatever reasons, food is perceived as less appetizing in dark rooms, and the rooms are also harder to keep clean.

Wallpaper can also be used in the kitchen, but use paper that is resistant to water, humidity, and moisture. Note that vinyl wallcovering is available in hundreds of patterns, many of which are ideally suited for kitchen applications. One of the most important things about applying wallpaper in the kitchen is ensuring that the base wall is properly prepared to accept wallpaper. There are numerous products available for sizing or otherwise preparing the wall.

Ceilings can be covered with paint, wallpaper, or a variety of acoustical coverings. The same guidelines governing the use of paint and wallpaper apply to the ceiling. The surface must be washable and able to withstand humidity and cooking grease. Another option, however, is to use *acoustical panels*, Fig. 4-15. These can be easily installed by just about anyone and provide a quick fix to an otherwise unattractive ceiling. Considering the noisy family life that goes on in a kitchen, it might be useful to install an acoustical ceiling just to deaden some of the noise.

REMODELING STRATEGIES

Of all the home remodeling projects that can be undertaken, improvements to the kitchen are perhaps the most common. It is easy to understand why once you realize how important the kitchen is to prospective home buyers. It is usually possible to recover a relatively high percentage of the cost of the remodeling project when you sell your house.

As pointed out earlier, the kitchen is one of the most complicated and complex rooms in the house, both aesthetically and functionally. Consequently, remodeling a kitchen is usually expensive. Typical costs for major kitchen renovation range from about $18,000 to nearly $25,000. Much of this cost is tied up in installing new cabinets and major appliances. Minor kitchen remodeling projects, on the other hand, generally can be accomplished for between $5,000 and $10,000. A major renovation might involve knocking out walls; adding skylights, doors, or windows; and installing expensive appliances and cabinets. Minor remodeling projects usually involve only replacing the cabinets, appliances, flooring, and painting.

Considering the high costs associated with kitchen renovations, you might wonder if it is worth the trouble and expense. For the most part it is. Estimates vary, but you can expect to recover anywhere from 70 to 90 percent of the renovation costs when selling the house. Major remodeling projects tend to return a greater percentage (that is, closer to 90 percent) than minor jobs (which are at the lower end). If you opt to do the work yourself—where the total cost of a minor renovation might be less than $4,000—you stand a good chance of recovering 100 percent or more.

More than one out of four home buyers say that they will remodel the kitchen themselves within the first year of owning a house. If you have already remodeled and brought your kitchen up-to-date, buyers will see this as one less area where they will have to invest time, money, and trouble.

It is very easy to invest too much money in a remodeled kitchen, particularly if you are planning on eventually selling the house. Instead of creating a luxurious, extravagant kitchen that is too personal, focus

Fig. 4-15. *A suspended acoustical tile ceiling hung above a kitchen (courtesy of Armstrong World Industries, Inc.).*

your resources on conveniences and design schemes that will appeal to a wide range of potential buyers. Select neutral colors and brand name, reliable appliances.

BUYER PREFERENCE

As Chapter 3 pointed out, about two-thirds of all home buyers indicate a strong preference for houses that have kitchens facing the backyard of the house. While shoppers haven't specified a precise size for the kitchen, a majority say that a large kitchen is one of the top two things they look at when evaluating a kitchen. The preferred layout among home shoppers is an L-shaped floor plan with either an island work area or a large space for a table, Fig. 4-16. (This eating space is in addition to a larger dining room.) Few buyers indicate a preference for a small eating area in the kitchen as being the only such area in the house.

Fig. 4-16. *An L-shaped floor plan with either an island work area or a large space for a table is preferred by many home buyers (courtesy of Armstrong World Industries, Inc.).*

When it comes to cabinets, more than three out of every four home shoppers want wooden cabinets that are finished in stained wood. The preferred stain is a medium darkness, somewhere darker than walnut but lighter than light oak. Ceramic tile countertops are the preference leader among buyers, although Corian-type countertops are gaining in popularity. Resilient floor covering is desired by almost three out of every four home shoppers.

By far the most sought after built-in appliance is a self-cleaning oven. That oven should be a single oven with a microwave. Homes with microwave ovens are becoming more the norm as more than one-third of all buyers say they will use a microwave. The preferred arrangement is a built-in single oven with a cooktop range plus a microwave. Other built-in appliances that shoppers expect a kitchen to have include a dishwasher (three out of every four buyers want one) and a garbage disposal (two out of every three expect this). Stainless steel sinks are also preferred by most buyers.

SERVICE AREAS

The kitchen isn't the only service area in the house. Along with it are rooms like the laundry or utility room, the garage, the basement, and various storage areas throughout the house. Because service areas aren't among the most glamorous rooms in a house, they are often overlooked, an oversight that home sellers sometimes find costly. First-time buyers in particular tend to be concerned about the condition of the service areas because any necessary repair or remodeling work in these areas is perceived as being expensive. Move-down buyers, on the other hand, are more concerned about service area storage facilities and labor-saving features.

When it comes to service areas other than the kitchen, the need for efficiency and cleanliness far outstrips the desire for aesthetics. Not only do service areas need to be laid out so that work can be accomplished easily, but the rooms must be logically positioned in regards to each other.

LAUNDRY ROOMS

Laundry facilities are usually provided in one of three or four parts of the house. In some instances, a washer and dryer are built into a closet in the bedroom section of the house. Some builders also try to place the laundry area in or near the bathroom, arguing that it makes more sense than placing the laundry near the kitchen.

The advantage of arrangements like this is primarily one of convenience. Having the laundry near the bedrooms and bathrooms can be handy. Laundry doesn't have to be lugged from one end of the house to the other before and after washing. Most laundry comes from the sleeping areas anyway and is stored there once it has been washed. On the negative side, however, such laundry facilities do have limitations.

If the appliance breaks down, repair is inconvenient and messy. Plus, the noise made by a washer or dryer can be disruptive to anyone sleeping in a nearby room.

For reasons like this, many homeowners prefer to have the laundry facilities located in a separate part of the house. The possible locations include the garage, basement, or separate laundry room. What is convenient about these areas is that they are often located near the kitchen, the number one work area in the house. Having the laundry and kitchen close to each other makes for efficient foot traffic—you don't have to walk so far back and forth when you work in both the kitchen and in the laundry area. Additionally, it is generally more efficient to lay the utility lines—water, gas, electric, and drain.

There are three other advantages to locating the laundry facilities away from the living quarters of the house. For one thing, such locations are typically well separated from the rest of the house, and family members won't be disrupted. Secondly, they usually provide easy outdoor access, making it convenient to carry laundry in and out to a clothesline. Finally, a separate laundry area usually provides enough work space for handwashing, ironing boards, hanging clothes, or other tasks that require additional space, Fig. 4-17. A dedicated area also provides space for storing soaps, cleansers, mops, and other cleaning tools.

UTILITY ROOMS

Laundry facilities are often placed in a utility room along with the furnace, water heater, and electrical service box. Such an arrangement generally does not pose a problem, although it makes the room more crowded and difficult to keep clean.

It is convenient to have the utility room in the basement if the house has one. Make sure, however, that there is easy access to the basement to and from the outside. If a new furnace or air conditioner has to be installed, for instance, the job will be easier if it isn't difficult to haul the bulky parts down into the basement.

STORAGE AREAS

The argument can be made that no house has ever had too much storage area. Nearly 90 percent of all home shoppers say that the amount of storage space in a house plays a very important part in their buying decision. Adequate storage space is more important to home shoppers who have owned homes before, probably because they have accumulated more household items and might have lived in a house that didn't have enough storage space.

You should plan adequate storage space in just about every room in the house. Also plan plenty of general-purpose storage space to store tools, extra utensils, seasonal clothes, and all the things people collect over time.

When there is enough pitch to the roof, attics are often used for storage. The biggest problem with using attics for storage is having easy access to the area. A set of stairs that go up to the attic is best, but few of today's homes can facilitate this. Second best, and more common in modern homes, is an attic door with fold-down steps. The garage or utility room is probably the best location for this kind of access. If the attic is used

Fig. 4-17. *Home shoppers prefer a separate laundry room that has enough space for related tasks such as sewing and ironing (courtesy of Whirlpool Corp.).*

74

for storage, be sure that the ceiling joists can support the additional weight. Install a storage surface or walking area so that you don't have to pick your way from joist to joist.

GARAGES

Garages tend to take on a life of their own. Although their fundamental purpose is to store automobiles, they often end up as exercise areas, family rooms, laundry rooms, storage areas, or all of the above.

The major trend in garage design since World War II has been the acceptance of attached garages. Few homes built today have detached garages. At the same time, there is little demand for single-car garages. Home shoppers want garages that have space for at least two cars, even if they only have one car. In such cases, the second bay offers an attractive storage or work area.

There are problems with attached garages. For one thing, the noise of cars entering and leaving the garage can be disruptive. The associated smell of carbon monoxide and gasoline fumes can be annoying, if not dangerous. Consequently, do not locate garages near bedrooms. You'll probably want the garage near the kitchen so that groceries can be conveniently carried into the house without being subject to inclement weather.

One of the major garage features that shoppers look for is an electric garage door opener. In most instances, automatic garage door openers are viewed as labor-saving devices. In other cases, buyers see them as a security device that enables homeowners to enter the garage without having to get out of the car.

REMODELING STRATEGIES

Service areas rank fairly low in importance when it comes to remodeling to enhance resale values. The only exception is the expansion of a one-car garage to one that stores two cars. A job such as this will probably cost between $5,000 and $10,000, and you can expect to recoup about 75 percent of the investment when you sell the house. If your property doesn't have a garage in the first place, you can generally expect to recover at least 100 percent of the cost upon selling the house. Fewer than 10 percent of home shoppers plan on spending much effort on remodeling or modernizing existing garages.

The other service area that home shoppers pay attention to is the basement. While certain cosmetic improvements such as adding vinyl flooring, wall paneling, and a suspended ceiling makes the basement less dungeonlike, it really doesn't add much to the resale value of the house. If you recover 30 percent of the cost, consider yourself lucky. In short, keep basement renovations to a minimum and, if at all possible, do the work yourself where your chances of recouping your investments are greater.

BUYER PREFERENCE

Neglected service areas can seriously impact the resale value of a house. While it isn't necessarily important to shoppers that service areas be particularly attractive (except for the kitchen, of course), it is important that the service areas be utilitarian in nature and efficient in design. Location of the individual areas, particularly in terms of how the location makes work easier, is of prime importance.

Laundry areas especially reflect the importance of location. Nearly three out of every four home shoppers have indicated they want laundry facilities in a separate room and that room should be adjacent to an attached garage. On the other hand, only about one out of five shoppers would accept closet-type laundry facilities near the bedroom, and only one out of ten find the kitchen a suitable location for the laundry. Having a separate laundry room is more important to move-up shoppers than first-time buyers, who are more willing to accept laundries in the garage.

Two-car garages are overwhelmingly the preferred layout. A surprisingly number of people indicate, however, that they want more room in the garage than just room to park a couple of cars. They feel the garage should provide additional room for storage, hobbies, or other activities.

Buyers don't mind if the furnace and water heater are located in the garage. In keeping with their desire for convenience and security, home shoppers really see automatic garage door openers as an attractive feature.

5

Bathrooms

BACK IN THE DAYS WHEN BATHROOMS WERE KNOWN AS WA-
ter closets, they really didn't have much influence over home shopper's
buying decisions. This has changed, however, and today the bathroom
is one of the Big Three rooms that shoppers evaluate when comparing
homes. One reason home shoppers pay so much attention to the bathroom is that it will be an expensive room for them to repair or remodel
if they believe they will eventually have to do so. Therefore, it is important
that you do whatever you can to present an attractive room that will not
make shoppers nervous.

Historically, bathrooms have been small in size. Nevertheless, their
wiring, plumbing, ventilation, fixtures, fittings, and special environmental
conditions have made them one of the most complicated rooms in a house.
Bathrooms fall into several categories, ranging from elaborate suites that
are attached to master bedrooms to small powder rooms tucked beneath
stairways. There is a wide diversity in the type of fixtures, fittings, styles,
and colors that are being used in today's baths. New homes are rarely
outfitted with the standard white porcelain fixtures and chromed fittings
that have graced homes over the past 100 years. By paying special

attention to the choice of fixtures, you can make the room more pleasing for yourself as well as future buyers.

When your home is eventually on the market, bathrooms provide you with a real opportunity to show off your house if the bathroom takes advantage of the many colorful and attractive fixtures that are available to homeowners. A plain, old-fashioned bathroom, even though it might be only a few years old, will not help your cause. Buyers will immediately realize that money might have to be spent later to remodel the room. New fixtures and fittings, even if they have an old-fashioned or traditional design, are important to buyers because they suggest low maintenance and convenience.

LAYOUT STRATEGIES

The size, shape, and positioning of fixtures (that is, bathtubs, lavatories, commodes, etc.) in bathrooms, particularly in those rooms that are relatively cramped, is very important. Design consideration must also be given to ensuring privacy, providing storage, and minimizing noise. It is clear that buyers are beginning to prefer that the largest, most elaborate bathroom in the house be attached to the master bedroom. With this in mind, the specific design of master suites and attached bathrooms will be covered in Chapter 6, which discusses bedroom design. If your house has more than one bathroom and you want to spend money on bath improvements, spend that money on the bath in the master suite.

There are a number of standard components that take up floor space in a bathroom and must be considered during the design stage. The basic components are tubs, basins, and toilets. Special situations might vary, such as the half-bath or powder room in Fig. 5-1 that has only a toilet and basin. A minimum full-size bath will also include a bathtub (or shower) and storage facilities. Beyond that, a bath can have both a shower and tub, a cabinet lavatory, dual basins, perhaps a bidet, a whirlpool, laundry hamper, and so on. Components to consider, but that usually don't require floor space, are mirrors, towel racks, soap dishes, etc. Finally, you must account and design for ventilation, windows, lighting, plumbing, and electricity.

DESIGN STRATEGIES

Depending on the size and shape of the available space, most bathrooms are designed using one of three basic layouts. The simplest layout is a *single-wall bathroom*. It is ideally suited for a long, narrow space where the lack of available width dictates that all components that require plumbing be located against one wall. Figure 5-2 illustrates what this type of bathroom might look like.

A variation of the one-wall bathroom is the L-shaped layout. In this design, the bathtub occupies the shorter leg of the L.

Fig. 5-1. *Typical powder room with basic bathroom fixtures (courtesy of Kohler Co.).*

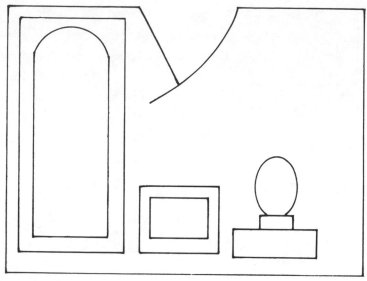

Fig. 5-2. *Single-wall bathroom layout.*

A *two-wall corridor bathroom*, on the other hand, is wide enough to accommodate fixtures positioned along opposing walls. In some instances, all the plumbing can be located along one wall, with storage and make-up facilities on the opposite wall. Allow a minimum of 30 inches between the opposing fixtures. As Fig. 5-3 shows, a two-wall bathroom will often be located between two bedrooms, with opposing doors providing access to the rooms. A third door can then be added to provide hall access, if appropriate.

If enough space is available, square rooms can be designed in a U-shape with all plumbing fixtures situated in the center of the room (Fig. 5-4). One advantage of this design is that it provides some degree of privacy.

A variation of the U-shaped design positions the fixtures along the walls instead of in the center. Distributing the plumbing along three walls requires more up-front work on the part of plumbers and carpenters, but the layout is comfortable and practical.

The style of the bathroom should reflect the overall style of the house itself. Because you have many more attractive options when it comes to style and color than there used to be, you might be tempted to choose a style of fixtures that makes a nice bathroom but doesn't fit with the rest of the house. A rustic country home might mean you use an oak vanity or pedestal basin and a claw-footed bathtub, like those used in the bathroom in Fig. 5-5.

Color selection should be one of the first things you consider when evaluating a bathroom, although finalizing the color scheme is sometimes

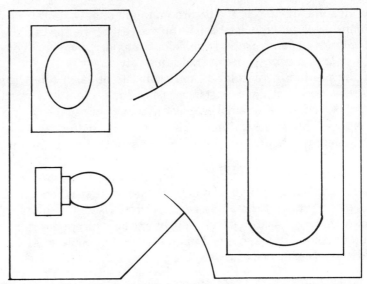

Fig. 5 3. *Two wall corridor bathroom layout.*

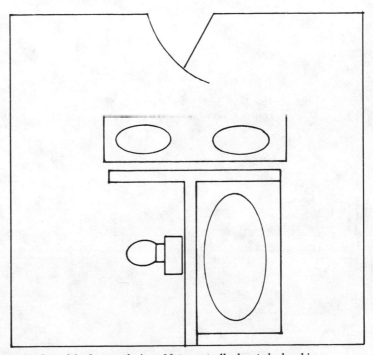

Fig. 5-4. U-*shaped bathroom design. Note centrally located plumbing.*

tricky. In some instances, the bathroom might simply conform to a predominant color scheme established by the rest of the house. The bathroom might not lend itself to the color scheme, however, even if it is designed to conform to the overall house style.

If the predominant color scheme consists of earth tones (browns, oranges, yellows, etc.), for instance, using such colors in a small room might make it seem even smaller. You can easily change the color of paint or wallpaper, but if the bathroom fixtures are a unique color, changing the entire color scheme later by you or an eventual buyer might be difficult.

Bathrooms that use complementary, somewhat neutral, colors that appeal to the widest range of home buyers are best when considering the resale potential, particularly with fixtures. Use light colors to make a room seem larger. Fixtures that are light in color will appear to be farther apart. (For color accents, depend upon easily replaceable accessories like soap dishes, towel racks, towels, etc.)

Fig. 5-5. *A rustic home decorated with antiques should have a bathroom like this one that matches the home's overall decor (courtesy of Merillat Industries, Inc.).*

Having enough storage throughout the house, and particularly in smaller rooms like bathrooms, is becoming more important to all home buyers. Nine out of ten home shoppers say that availability of storage space in the bathroom is an important factor when evaluating at a house. And it shouldn't be surprising that storage space is more important to move-down buyers or empty nesters who have had a lifetime to accumulate household goods than to younger buyers.

Consequently, every bathroom should have some sort of storage facilities, even if those facilities are minimal. For full-size baths (Fig. 5-6), set aside space for linens, toiletries, etc. Linen storage requires a cabinet or closet, while toiletries can be stored in a vanity, preferably in drawers. If space permits, a clothes hamper is often desired as well. Medicine cabinets usually don't take up any floor space. If your bathroom doesn't have a medicine cabinet, provide some space to safely store potentially harmful medicines away from small children.

Fig. 5-6. *Having adequate storage space like that offered in this bathroom is very important to home shoppers (courtesy of Kohler Co.).*

Keep in mind how many people will be using a particular bathroom and who they are. In a central bathroom used by several members of the family, allow adequate storage space for each individual. Set aside a vanity drawer or closet shelf per person. Two people will usually be the only ones using a bathroom attached to a master suite, so allocate storage space accordingly. Also set aside space for bathroom appliances—hair dryers, water pics, electric toothbrushes, etc.—that might be used. If necessary, store appliances as close to the electrical outlets as possible.

Because storage space is always at a premium, you will want to be as efficient as possible when designing it. Closet space, for instance, that is slightly too wide will collect clutter; space that is too narrow will be useless. When determining the shelf width, measure a folded bath towel and base the shelf on multiples of that. Do the same with other storage facilities.

SURFACE CONSIDERATIONS

The surface of a bathroom includes the floor, walls, and ceiling of the room and countertops on the vanities. Because the environment of the bathroom is *moisture intensive*, it must be treated differently than other rooms of the house.

Coping with Moisture

The moisture-laden environment in a bathroom cannot be overemphasized. It must be considered before the walls are erected and flooring laid down. Not only will water be spilled and splashed on the walls, but moisture trapped inside the room can cause mildew and mold to appear and drywall to disintegrate.

If you are building or remodeling your bathroom, you should ensure that the drywall itself, particularly around tubs and showers, is a special moisture-resistant material. Ask for it at your lumberyard and check for the letters *MR* or *WR* (for water-resistant). The paper covering the gypsum board will be green or blue color. Installation of moisture-resistant gypsum requires rustproof nails and special edge sealers. Check with your lumberyard for specifics.

If you are buying a used house, check for mildew or soft, damp spots on the walls. If you are buying a new house, be sure and ask the developer what sort of wallboard was used. Because moisture-resistant wallboard costs a little more than standard gypsum, some builders might try to cut corners here.

Covering the Walls

Once the wallboard is up, it is most often covered with paint, wallpaper, tile, or plastic panels. (Some painters recommend that paint or wallpaper not be applied on top of water-resistant wallboard. Check with your lumberyard or paint store for specific application information.)

When *painting* a bathroom, use a water-based, washable, moisture/mildew-resistant, acrylic-latex paint for walls and ceilings. For woodwork, use an alkyd interior/exterior enamel. Avoid flat paints in bathrooms because they are less resistant to water and can't be washed as easily. Acrylic-enamel paint offers the greatest washability. Select a color that accents and enhances the bathroom fixtures.

If you opt to cover the walls with *wallpaper*, a vinyl-coated paper is the best. In most cases, standard wallpaper is usually too susceptible to moisture damage for use in a bathroom. To apply wallpaper in a bathroom, you'll probably want to use special high-strength adhesives or paste that are designed to withstand exposure to excessive moisture and steam. The adhesive on many standard prepasted wallpapers isn't strong enough. If you are making your own paste, you can add high-strength additives to compensate for moisture.

One of the most popular and practical bathroom wall coverings that home shoppers prefer is *ceramic tile*. It is usually installed wherever water comes in contact with the wall, particularly around plumbing fittings. While ceramic tile is usually the most difficult and expensive to install, it is considered the most durable. Ceramic tiles are available in hundreds of solid-color shades as well as in silk-screened patterns. Some manufacturers even make ceramic tiles that are pattern- and color-coordinated with bathroom fixtures like pedestal sinks and bathtubs.

Ceramic tiles used on the wall aren't the same as those used as flooring, although matching patterns can be selected. Most wall tiles are made from a white-body base and decorated with a colored glaze. The glaze is usually either a shiny or matte finish that is about ¼ inch in thickness. Use ceramic tiles that are as moisture-resistant as possible. Those that have a water-absorption level of 3 percent or less are best.

Equally as important as the tile itself is the *grout*, the material that fills the spaces between tiles. It is essential that you use a high-quality grout and that you apply it carefully and properly, otherwise water can get behind the tiles and ruin the wall. Because grout is available in dozens of colors, it serves an important decorative function too. Special mildew-resistant grouts also can be purchased.

Most of today's home shoppers tend to prefer ceramic tiles that are either very small (2 × 2 inches) or very large (12 × 12 inches) in size. Generally, the smaller size tiles can be used on both the wall and floor. Larger tiles are used on the floor only, with matching smaller tiles applied to the wall.

Another type of popular wallcovering is the *plastic-coated hardboard (masonite) panel*. These panels come in 4-×-8-foot sheets and usually have decorative patterns that resemble a variety of finishes, including everything from ceramic tiles to wood-grain paneling. The panels, which are attached to the gypsum wallboards with glue, are relatively easy to install, especially when compared to tile.

Which wallcovering do most home shoppers prefer? For the most part, they prefer a combination of ceramic tile and paint, or ceramic tile and vinyl wallpaper like the bathroom shown in Fig. 5-7. Although ceramic tile is perhaps the most dramatic, most buyers feel that an entire home bathroom finished in tile is too institutional for comfort. There is also no real reason for the entire room to be finished in tile. What is important is that the structure be protected from the moisture that is present in the bathroom. If the appearance of the room can be enhanced in the process, so much the better.

Don't forget that ceramic tile on the wall has the same cosmetic drawback that the fixtures in general have. That is, it is difficult to change the color or style to fit individual preferences. While you can recover a wallpapered wall and repaint a painted wall, all you can do with a ceramic tile wall to change a color or pattern is tear out the old tile and start over, an expensive and difficult process. Consequently, if you are

Fig. 5-7. *Ceramic tile floors in the bathroom are preferred by most home buyers (courtesy of Kohler Co.).*

choosing the color and pattern of ceramic tile and are concerned about its effect on the eventual resale of the house, choose a high-quality tile that is somewhat neutral and that corresponds with the color of the bathroom fixtures.

Flooring

When it comes to floors, it is very important that whatever type you use, it must have a nonskid surface because moisture and water that collects on the floor can cause a potentially hazardous situation. Of secondary importance is how cold the floor covering is, particularly in northern climates.

Bathroom carpets are usually both warm and skidproof. Don't use the same type of carpet that is used in other areas of the house, however. Standard carpets just won't stand up to the heavy moisture found in bathroom environments. Unlike conventional carpets that have a porous, moisture-absorbing backing, carpets used in bathrooms should be totally synthetic with a waterproof backing. Avoid synthetic indoor-outdoor carpet unless you are sure the backing is waterproof.

Vinyl flooring, both in sheet and tile form, is an attractive alternative covering for bathroom environments. This flooring is often referred to as *resilient flooring*, a term that describes its resistance to damage as opposed to the material it is made from. Resilient flooring consists of two basic layers, a pattern layer and a protective wear layer. The thicker the wear layer, the higher the quality of the flooring itself.

A variation of vinyl flooring is *cushioned sheet flooring* that comes in rolls from 6 to 15 feet in width. This three-ply covering material has a layer of resilient foam sandwiched between the pattern layer and the wear layer. Not only is this material comfortable to walk on, but it resists scratches and dents more than noncushioned flooring.

Vinyl tiles are another alternative, and except for their 12- × -12-inch size, they have many of the same properties as sheet vinyl. Vinyl tiles have the same multilayer structure and are somewhat easier, not more time-consuming, to install. Many of today's tiles have preapplied adhesive, so all you have to do is peel off the backing and press the panel onto the floor.

Ceramic tile is another floor covering that is often preferred for its durability and attractiveness. Ceramic tiles often cost more, but they require less upkeep and last virtually a lifetime. Tiles that go on the floor are different from tiles that go on walls. Floor tiles, like those in Fig. 5-8, are typically thicker and usually coated with a nonskid surface. This traction is created by adding an abrasive grit to the tile surface. Some glazed floor tiles are rated for their abrasion resistance qualities. Use tiles rated ''3'' or higher in high-traffic areas. For light traffic, you can get by with a rating of ''2.''

Countertops

Vanity countertops can be of a variety of materials. Plastic laminate is generally used at the low end, while ceramic tile or marble is considered an expensive or high-end option (Fig. 5-9). Additionally, many bathrooms now have countertops made from Corian or other synthetic materials (Fig. 5-10).

If you have a choice, select the most waterproof surface material possible. Even relatively expensive plastic laminate tends to come unglued from the undersurface after a number of years. Particularly attractive to buyers are one-piece countertops/sinks that are typically made from Corian.

FIXTURES AND FITTINGS

The plumbing fixtures—tubs, lavatories, showers, toilets, vanities, etc.—used in a bathroom are both functional and decorative. In the past,

Fig. 5-8. *Home shoppers favor bathrooms with wallpaper and ceramic tile covering (courtesy of Merillat Industries, Inc.).*

bathroom fixtures came in only a few styles and a single color—white. Today's fixtures come in a variety of shapes, sizes, patterns, materials, and colors, making the selection process much more complicated than it used to be. One problem this wide variety presents for homeowners and remodelers, however, is that many of the newer fixtures have a modern, almost space-age look. Although they are attractive, they sometimes don't fit the overall design of traditional homes. For those homes that do have a more traditional design, middle-of-the-road and reproduction Victorian plumbing fixtures and fittings are available.

Years ago, plumbing fixtures like lavatories and tubs were made from cast iron that were enameled or coated with porcelain or powdered glass. Toilets were made from clay-based glazed vitreous china. Today, fixtures are made from a variety of materials, including enameled steel, acrylic, and fiberglass-reinforced plastic.

In most instances, the actual material used to make the fixture is of less importance to home buyers than the quality and style of the fixture,

Fig. 5-9. *Ceramic tile vanity countertops are popular with many shoppers (courtesy of Merillat Industries, Inc.).*

particularly quality. Home shoppers have expressed a desire for high-quality bathroom fixtures. They don't want noisy plumbing or lightweight bathtubs that have a ''spring'' to them when weight is applied. They don't want to go to the trouble, mess, and expense necessary to replace a cheap toilet or tub that has cracked or split.

How do you determine the relative quality of two different fixtures? One way is by price. Although higher quality fixtures are usually more expensive than lower quality items, you shouldn't automatically assume a direct relationship between cost and quality of the fixture. Often the additional cost is for the glossy finish. Look for water-resistant finishes that are impervious to abrasive cleaning materials used in bathrooms.Deal with brand name companies that have a wide selection and known history. Look for hairline cracks and imperfections or irregularities in the finish of lower quality fixtures. More importantly, look beyond the finish and find out what makes up the base material of the fixture.

Fig. 5-10. *Vanity countertops made from Corian are preferred by a majority of home shoppers (courtesy of DuPont Co.).*

This isn't to say that all fixtures must be cast iron. Certainly many enameled steel basins, fiberglass bathtubs, and synthetic lavatories are strong and can be of high quality. Furthermore, fiberglass-reinforced and plastic materials provide attractive molded designs that aren't possible with traditional materials. In addition to the design, plastic and fiberglass fixtures are often lighter in weight and less expensive than others. Neither are they subject to corrosion and rust from the water itself. When comparing fixtures made from these materials, look for ones that are thick, well-trimmed, and have a uniformly coated surface.

Bathtubs and Showers

Bathtub styles have undergone a dramatic change over the last few years because homeowners are demanding bathtubs with more comfortable and functional shapes. Virtually all types of tubs can be found in recessed or corner room designs and for left-hand or right-hand apron installations. The most important evaluation of a tub is its size—home shoppers want as large a tub as the room design allows. It is also important, and sometimes required by building codes, that bathtubs have slip-resistant surfaces for safety.

Although they are still the most widely used, conventional *rectangular tubs* are beginning to fall into disfavor among home shoppers. Instead, buyers are expressing a preference for either square or platform/sunken tubs (Fig. 5-11). *Platform/sunken tubs* are usually built into a platform above the floor surface. The size and shape of the actual tub varies, however, they enable a wide variety of design alternatives, including fitting locations. Sunken tubs are rarely used in second-floor bathrooms. Whirlpool bathtubs, like the sunken tub in Fig. 5-12, are also becoming popular.

Home buyers are finding *square tubs*, which are typically 4 × 4 feet in size, very attractive because the fixtures offer a great deal of design and use flexibility. These tubs often have a seating ledge that is not only comfortable but also useful for handicapped or elderly individuals. Additionally, square tubs can be easily adapted for use as showers, particularly when a shallow square tub (called a *receptor tub*) is used. Most home shoppers still prefer separate tub and shower facilities, however.

Tub/shower combinations, sometimes called *integral tubs*, are large molded fiberglass units that serve as both a shower stall and bathtub. They're nice in that they provide a one-piece sealed unit that can quickly be put in place. They might, however, be somewhat difficult for home remodelers to get into a relatively small bathroom because of the unit's size. In most instances, the integral unit is moved into homes that are under construction before the framing and walls are complete; the bathroom is then built around the combination unit. In the same sense, it is difficult to remove an integral unit from an existing bathroom during remodeling without breaking it up into smaller pieces. Some manufacturers provide multipiece integral tubs that have separate wall panels for easier installation.

Showers continue to be in demand, particularly in homes that have more than two bathrooms. Most home shoppers prefer separate tub and shower stalls, especially in those bathrooms that are part of the master suite. Having tub/shower combinations is acceptable and, at least for secondary bathrooms, is even preferable to stall showers. In most instances, home buyers want to have a master bath with separate tub and shower units, with a combined tub/shower in the secondary bathroom.

As with bathtubs, most buyers prefer large, roomy shower stalls that are a minimum of 3-foot square. Except for one-piece shower stalls that have walls made from molded acrylic or fiberglass, like that shown in Fig. 5-13, a majority of the shower stalls are built at the site, with ceramic tile being the preferred wall material. (The wall is often referred to as the

Fig. 5-11. *Modern platform bathtubs are becoming increasingly popular with home buyers (courtesy of DuPont Co.).*

shower surround.) The bases (or floor pans) of such showers are usually made from fiberglass, cast masonry, terrazzo, or acrylic and designed for rectangular, square, or corner installation, all with nonslip surfacing.

The two complaints homeowners most often express about the quality of shower stall material and installation revolve around water leaks, which is an installation issue, and noise, which is a material issue. Proper and careful installation can prevent leaks. The noise of water hitting the walls of lightweight fiberglass or metal stalls is a nuisance, hence buyer preference for ceramic tile walls. If you install a lightweight shower stall, be sure it is amply insulated and supported to prevent noise.

Toilets

For the most part, the exact style of *toilet* doesn't matter to home buyers as long as the fixture matches the style and design of the other fixtures. Sometimes a buyer will prefer a *wall-mounted toilet* over a floor-

Fig. 5-12. *This sunken bathtub is a whirlpool bath (courtesy of Kohler Co.).*

mounted unit simply because it makes cleaning the floor an easier task. Nevertheless, *floor-mounted toilets* are more widely used in standard home construction because floor-mounted units do not have the special structural support and plumbing requirements needed by wall-mounted units. Of the floor-mounted toilets, the most popular style is the low-profile, one-piece devices like that in Fig. 5-14.

One thing that is of importance to many home buyers, particularly those in drier climates, is the amount of water a toilet uses. Every time a standard toilet is flushed, nearly 10 gallons of water goes down the drain. To conserve resources, fixture manufacturers have developed *water-saving toilets* that use less than 5 gallons for flushing. In some communities, building codes require these units in all newly constructed homes.

Homes that have bathrooms designed with the elderly or the handi-capped in mind will have a selling edge over the coming years. Taller

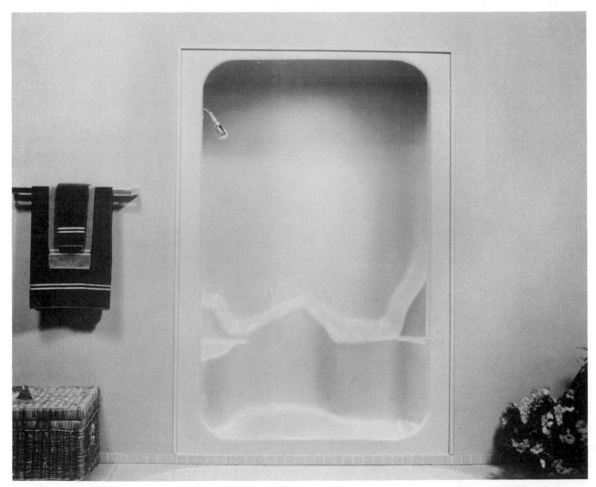

Fig. 5-13. *One-piece showers made from acrylic are favored by many home shoppers (courtesy of Kohler Co.).*

toilets for individuals who use wheelchairs or otherwise need special assistance are available. While the seat of most standard toilets averages about 12 inches off the floor, special toilets are about 18 inches high. Keep this in mind when selecting a wall-mounted or floor-mounted toilet. The height of wall-mounted units cannot be easily adjusted without tearing out the wall and associated plumbing. The height of floor-mounted toilets can be easily adjusted by simply installing a higher floor-mounted fixture. If any elderly or handicapped home buyer is evaluating your house, this will be one thing they will take into consideration.

Although the actual operating mechanism for a toilet is important in terms of noise and efficiency, most home buyers will never ask if a toilet is *washdown*, *reverse trap*, or *siphon action*. Functionally, the difference between them is in the amount of noise, amount of water, and capability not to clog up. (Siphon action toilets are perhaps the best—and the most expensive.)

Fig. 5-14. *Home buyers generally prefer low-profile, one-piece floor-mounted toilets (courtesy of Merillat Industries, Inc.).*

Sinks

Lavatory sinks come in three basic configurations: wall-hung basins, vanity-mounted countertops, and pedestal sinks. While home buyers don't mind small, *wall-hung basins* (Fig. 5-15) in compact powder rooms, the expressed preference by shoppers, particularly in bathrooms attached to master suites, is for dual-basin units. To satisfy this demand, some manufacturers provide *single unit, dual-basin countertops* (Fig. 5-16).

Although antique pedestal sinks were free-standing, today's *pedestal sinks* have slender but weak pedestals (Figs. 5-17 and 5-18). They are therefore usually supported by hanging the unit from the wall.

Vanity Cabinets

The primary function of *vanity cabinets* is to provide a countertop work area in the bathroom. Vanities also provide under-the-counter storage,

Fig. 5-15. *Small, wall-hung basins are commonly used in powder rooms (courtesy of Porcher, Inc.).*

hide plumbing, and enhance the general appearance of the room. The style of vanities varies tremendously, but again, should be consistent first with the design of the bathroom and then with the overall design of the house.

When it comes to the material used for vanity tops, *ceramic tile* is what home buyers like to see most often. No matter what material the countertop is, however, it is imperative that the top be waterproof and stain resistant. Increasingly, home builders are turning to molded countertops made from synthetic materials like DuPont's *Corian*.

Younger home buyers with small children will look favorably on vanities that have at least one cabinet door or drawer that has a keyed lock. This will enable them to keep potentially hazardous cleansers or medicines safely away from youngsters.

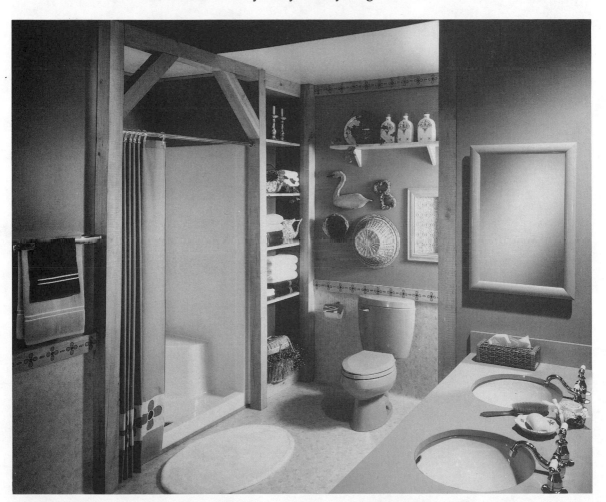

Fig. 5-16. *Dual-basin vanities are preferred by most home buyers (courtesy of Kohler Co.).*

Fig. 5-17. *Modern pedastal basins are often supported from the wall as well as by the stand (courtesy of Kohler Co.).*

Fig. 5-18. *Console pedastal basins have a more traditional look (courtesy of Kohler Co.).*

Fittings

Bathroom *fittings* are the knobs, faucets, and drain mechanisms that attach to fixtures and make them useful. The first thing home buyers notice about fittings is their appearance. In the past couple of years, manufacturers have begun designing stylistic fittings (Fig. 5-19) using a variety of materials, all of which are a far cry from the nickel and chrome-plated faucets of past years.

When it comes to fittings, quality is extremely important because cheaply made fittings will wear quickly, both internally and externally. Brass fittings, plated with chrome or gold, are the best choice because they are long wearing and resistant to corrosion. And many of the fittings have easy-to-replace cartridgelike mechanisms that replace the conventional washer mechanism of older faucets.

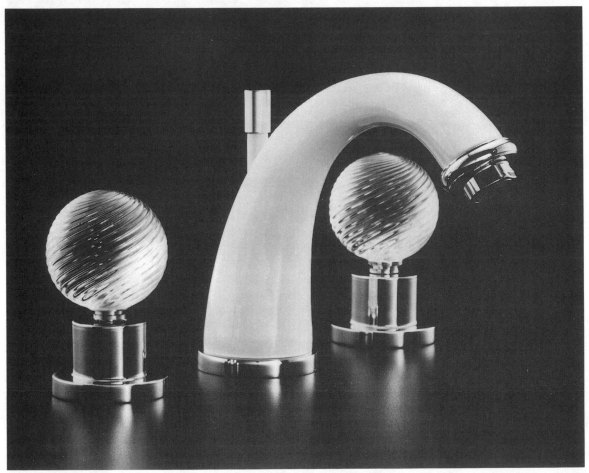

Fig. 5-19. *An example of modern bathroom fittings (courtesy of Kohler Co.).*

LIGHTING

Bathrooms present lighting challenges not faced by other rooms in the house. For one thing, most bathrooms have little access to natural light because the room typically only has a single window, and a small one at that. Consequently, a bathroom filled with thousands of dollars of fixtures and fittings can appear far less striking than intended simply because of inadequate lighting. This is one reason why it is important to correctly identify the location of the bathroom during the design phase. In addition to providing a more enjoyable effect, taking advantage of the sun's natural light can save energy and money during daytime use. *Glass bricks*, like those used in the bathroom in Fig. 5-20, can often let in much

Fig. 5-20. *Glass tiles used instead of standard windows can allow you to take greater advantage of natural light (courtesy of Merillat Industries, Inc.).*

more natural light than regular windows, and when used in conjunction with artificial light, can provide a nice effect.

Another contributing factor to the complex issue of bathroom lighting is that several types of activities, each with different lighting requirements, take place in the bathroom every day. Often times, people prefer bright lights for stimulation in the morning when they are getting ready for the day, but softer, subdued lights that are more calming in the evening when they are relaxing in a hot bath.

Applying makeup requires direct, but shadow-free, lighting from multiple 120- to 180-watt incandescent bulbs. Light that illuminates tub or shower, however, should come from 60- or 75-watt incandescent bulbs that are used with vapor- or moisture-proof light fixtures.

Light-colored bathrooms and those with a large number of mirrors appear larger in size and require less light than dark-colored bathrooms with few mirrors. When planning lighting strategies for bathrooms, remember that while incandescent lights provide the warmest, nonharsh tones enjoyed by most people, they also cast a yellowish tint. On the other hand, fluorescent lights provide a cool, blue tint that you should avoid in bathrooms unless they are precisely planned for. The final lighting scheme consist of a mixture of the two.

Remember that bathrooms can be dangerous, especially when water is spilled on ceramic tile floors. In such an environment, it is even more crucial that you provide adequate lighting.

REMODELING STRATEGIES

Old-looking, out-of-date bathrooms detract from the selling value of a home. A bright, modern bathroom, with a vanity instead of just a sink for instance, can be a big attraction. The bathroom consistently is one of the rooms that is most often renovated. More than one out of four home buyers say that they will remodel the main bathroom within the first year of owning a house.

Because the bathroom is so important, recovering the cost of a bathroom addition is usually no problem as long as the bathroom isn't overly improved or remodeled with obviously poor quality materials. Investment return upon the sale of the house typically runs about 110 to 120 percent. This means that adding a full bathroom is one of the few remodeling items that you will actually make money on. When fully contracted out, a bathroom addition can cost as much as $7,300. When you sell the house, however, the additional bathroom value is about $8,000.

Some estimates place a bathroom addition that involves adding space costs at about $8,500. If you simply renovate a room and use existing walls, the cost will be about $7,000. Renovating a closet to create a powder room will cost about $5,000. In each case, you will recoup 100 percent of the investment.

Bathroom remodeling is another thing. In most instances, it will cost between $3,000 and $6,000 to remodel a bathroom. On a square foot basis, it usually costs more to remodel a bathroom than to build a new one from scratch. From 75 to 100 percent of the investment will be returned on bathroom renovations, however. Some estimates place bathroom remodeling at only a 56 percent recovery. Inexpensive fixtures, such as fiberglass tubs, can have a negative effect if the buyer perceives them as a cheap, cosmetic replacement.

One minor renovation in the bathroom simply involves the replacement of fittings and other accessories such as towel racks and soap dishes. For a minimum cost and effort, an old bathroom can be livened up quite a bit. (Faucets that are too fancy, however, might scare some buyers because they appear to require more cleaning and polishing than standard units.)

BUYER PREFERENCE

The first question most home shoppers ask about bathrooms is "How many bathrooms does the house have?" More than half of all home shoppers, including both first-time and move-up buyers, prefer a house that has at least two baths. Having multiple bathrooms is more important to move-up buyers who often have adolescent children and need both more room and privacy. Having additional bathrooms appears to be one of the main reasons move-up buyers want another house as virtually no move-up buyers polled in surveys indicate they want a house with only a single bathroom.

As a rule, plan on a house having at least one bathroom for every two bedrooms. Because, as discussed in Chapter 3, nearly 75 percent of all home shoppers prefer homes with three or four bedrooms, two baths is the obvious minimum.

Professional home builders have recognized this trend. In 1950, only 8 percent of the new homes built in the United States had two or more bathrooms. Today, 82 percent of the homes built for sale have two or more bathrooms, a statistic that points out the importance home buyers place upon the number of bathrooms.

Although two bathrooms is the minimum requirement for most people, a growing number of shoppers are demanding homes that have two-and-a-half baths, particularly in two-story homes with master suites. Unlike home buyers of a few years ago who were satisfied with a full-size bath that served the entire house and a half-size bath attached to the master bedroom, today's home shoppers prefer to have the most elaborate bathroom in the house attached to the master suite. They then want a second bath available for the other bedrooms, with a half-bath (or powder room) installed near the living or family area of the house.

After the number of bathrooms in a house, home shoppers are most concerned about the size of the bathrooms. This is important not only for simply having enough room to move around in, but also for being large enough to include desired features. In the past, the size of bathrooms was dictated by the size of the bathtub, which is usually the largest fixture in the room. Traditionally, bathrooms were about 5 × 7 feet in size, which stemmed from 5-foot long tubs. As manufacturers began offering larger tubs that appealed to homeowners, however, the size of the bathrooms necessarily had to grow.

The minimum size for a bathroom is generally no less than 6 × 8 feet. Note that this is the recommended minimum and that elaborate baths require much more space. A 6-×-8-foot bath will accommodate a small closet, toilet, tub/shower combination, and a dual-basin lavatory. Sometimes, a 5-×-7-foot bathroom or powder room is acceptable if it is well-designed. If a tub or shower is included in a 5-×-7-foot bathroom, it is usually located along the 5-foot wall.

There are a number of factors that influence bathroom size, among them the basic size of fixtures and the amount of clearance between them. As a general rule, two people should be able to move about at once in the bathroom. This requires a minimum of 30 inches of space between fixtures.

Care must also be taken that there is adequate room to open doors to closets, vanities, showers, and even the entry door. Because you might someday sell the house to an elderly or handicapped person, you might want to ensure that bathrooms, particularly those on the ground floor, have room for wall-mounted handrails and wheelchair access. Over the next few years, handrails will become more important in both bathrooms and hallways as the general population grows older. Features that accommodate the needs of the elderly will be a major home selling point over the coming years. In the same sense, larger bathrooms are often being used to accommodate exercise or rehabilitation equipment.

The floor plan of the preferred two-story, two-and-a-half bathroom home is to have a master bath just off the master bedroom. A second bath would then be shared between the other bedrooms. In such a house, the first floor would have a relatively small (5-×-7-foot) powder room with a basin and commode. It is also a good idea to compartmentalize powder rooms and half-baths so a door separates the vanity and basin from the toilet. This way, two people can have access to the room at once.

The bathroom off the master bedroom should have a dual-basin vanity with a ceramic tile or Corian countertop (this is the most preferred feature) and an oversize tub with a separate shower with ceramic tile surround. A trend is to include a spa tub in the master suite. Note that master baths can accommodate vanities up to 36 inches high. This height is higher than the standard 30-inch countertop but is acceptable because you safely assume that vanities in the master bath will only be used by adults. Having a higher vanity can prevent back problems and other inconveniences of bending over a low basin.

6

Bedrooms and Personal Living Areas

Shopping for a home is, to a large extent, a process of elimination. Although most buyers look at a number of houses in their search for the "right" home, they end up getting serious about only a few. With the exception of location, the most important thing about a specific house that provides the initial basis for elimination or acceptance is the bedroom—more precisely the number of bedrooms. Simply open a newspaper to the real estate section and you'll see that houses are first categorized according to geographic location and to the number of bedrooms. Homeowners are quick to realize the importance that home buyers place on the number of bedrooms. They often go to great extents to add those rooms, even to converting garages and basements.

One reason why bedrooms are considered so important is that their primary use is for sleeping, and sleep is one activity that takes place in a certain place at a certain time and requires a minimum space. Members of a family often eat at different times, so a large dining room or kitchen might not be crucial. Family members might not all watch TV or read in the same room at the same time, so a large family or living room might not be mandatory. Most members of the family will congregate in their

Fig. 6-1. *Bedrooms often provide personal places where you can read or write letters in private (courtesy of Armstrong World Industries, Inc.).*

bedrooms at the same time, however, and an adequate number of bedrooms, defined by the size of the family, must be available.

As with many other aspects of today's homes, the perception and role of the bedroom has changed. To a large part, this change is because of the shifting life-styles of homeowners who typically want to spend more time at home and want more privacy while there. In addition to a place just to sleep, homeowners now want a space to relax, a quiet room for reading or writing letters (Fig. 6-1), a personal place just to get away. The bedroom is a natural candidate for providing this privacy. For many people, the bedroom has become the center of home-oriented activities, with today's homeowners spending more than one-third of their home life in the bedroom.

Move-up buyers, in particular, indicate that they see themselves spending more time at home than ever before, particularly if the house is designed with amenities conducive to home-oriented activities. One reason for this is that many move-up buyers have school-age children living at home. Still, three out of four first-time buyers and empty nesters spend more evenings at home than previously.

While life-style patterns such as these have an undeniable impact on informal living areas of the house, their impact on bedroom areas is perhaps even greater. Many of today's master bedrooms have become suites that are often one of the largest living areas in the house and include spas, exercise facilities, full-baths, and extensive storage space. Obviously, the change in the role and design of the bedroom reflects a change in the way people will live over the coming years. With this in mind, it should come as no surprise that, with kitchens and bathrooms, the design and number of a house's bedrooms are a major factor influencing the buying decision of virtually all of today's home shoppers.

LAYOUT STRATEGIES

If the main function of the bedroom were simply to provide space for sleeping, a simple boxlike room design would suffice. Personalizing the room would then be a matter of decorating, not one of layout and design. Because today's bedrooms are usually multifunctional, the layout, design, and decorating are all equally important.

The simplest approach is to design a large open room that will provide future occupants with the flexibility to adapt the room to their own life-styles and decorating schemes. Buyers will naturally want to create their own personalized areas, and an open design makes this possible. Open areas allow a variety of decorating options, including the addition of divider walls, large pieces of furniture, and the clear delineation of functional areas.

Not only do you need to know the various decorating options that are available (atrium doors, mirrored wardrobes, etc.), you also must account for functions that will require floor space. These functional areas include bathing, clothing and bedding storage, and entertainment, in addition to sleeping.

As Fig. 6-2 illustrates, the bed is the one object that usually takes up most of the floor space in a bedroom. After that, storage areas, both drawers and hanging space for clothing, take up the most floor space. Many home shoppers are now also looking for enough room in the master bedroom to use exercise equipment. Consequently, the more room the master bedroom has, the better off you will be when showing the house to home shoppers.

DESIGN STRATEGIES

When considering how to lay out a bedroom, keep in mind that there are several different approaches to designing such a room. If your house has a balcony or patio, the bedroom can easily be turned into a *garden bedroom* (sometimes called a *Florida room*). While this design was at one time popular only in warmer climates like Florida, the Southwest, and Southern California, the emergence of greenhouses and solariums for homes, as well as highly insulated sliding glass doors and floor-to-ceiling

Fig. 6-2. *Beds usually take up more floor space in the bedroom than any other piece of furniture (courtesy of Sears, Roebuck, & Co.).*

windows, has extended the garden bedroom concept across the country. Smaller, secondary bedrooms that are not large enough for a sitting area often benefit from having a balcony or patio opening on the outside to extend the living area.

Even if you don't develop the indoor/outdoor bedroom area yourself, the large window will make the room appear larger to prospective buyers who can easily see the possibilities in such a room. If you live in a region of the country that experiences cold winters, however, a poorly insulated garden bedroom might turn buyers away. Note that more shoppers prefer balconies or patios in the bedroom than sitting rooms and fireplaces.

Guest bedrooms, particularly those that double as another room in real life, are often the most forgotten room in the house. They tend to be a magnet for any odds and ends that are too good to be relegated to the garage, but not good enough to be kept in the house proper. The room might not be decorated in keeping with the rest of the house either. Rooms like this are generally uncomfortable for guests who might be staying with you and unappealing to home shoppers who are evaluating the house.

What can you do with the guest room to make it attractive to both guests and potential buyers? For one thing, consider using a Murphy bed or hide-a-bed instead of a regular bed in the room. This will let you use the room as something other than a bedroom, yet still let you quickly convert the room to serve that purpose. It is important that the decor of the guest room be a natural extension of the decor in the rest of the house, even if it is normally used as a sewing room, office, or whatever. Guest rooms normally don't need as much closet space as normal bedrooms, but some sort of closet space should be there. Its location should also allow access to a bathroom without having to walk through a communal area (like the kitchen) of the house.

Storage Considerations

Next to the bed, storage areas usually take up more space in the bedroom than anything else. This is the way it should be because home buyers have said that they like homes with lots of storage space.

Closets are the most common hanging storage areas. Unless the closet space is large enough for you to comfortably walk into, do not use standard doorways like those that allow entry into the bedroom. Closets that take up an entire wall should have accordion-type, sliding, or pocket doors so that inhabitants have straightforward access to the entire storage area, not just one part of it. Make sure the closets are deep enough to allow all sorts of clothing to be hung without getting wrinkled. Allow a minimum of 6 to 8 linear feet of hanging closet space for each person who uses the room. Allow even more hanging space in closets in the master suite, at least 8 or 9 feet in smaller homes and up to 20 feet in larger houses. Shelf space in the closet should also be easily accessible.

Built-in storage systems, both closet space and chests of drawers (Fig. 6-3), are attractive. They tend to be decor-specific, however, matching the bedstead and pieces of furniture, and therefore less flexible. If someone buys the house and doesn't like the built-in chests that you installed (or even if you decide to change your decorating scheme), the built-in units might have to be torn out.

For bedrooms that are cramped in space, one alternative is to install a closet "carousel" similar to those found in professional dry-cleaning establishments. Such a system (Fig. 6-4) can save as much as 40 to 50 square feet of floor space. These systems, which usually have about 40 feet of hanging space, are almost always powered by standard electrical current and have a push-button wall switch. Because a power carousel enables you to use areas of the closet that are traditionally inaccessible, you can store more clothes in a small area.

On the other hand, *free-standing storage units* (wardrobes, amoires, chests, etc.) are less prone to personal design and are less likely to take efficient advantage of available floor space. Free-standing units are portable, however, allowing you to easily change the design of the room or take with you when you sell the house.

By attaching *mirrors* to either the interior or exterior of closet doors, you can put that door to double use. Mirrors on the exterior of closet doors also open up the room and make it seem somewhat larger.

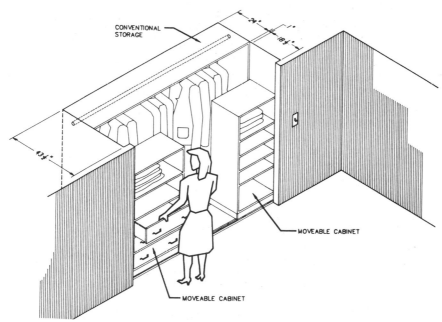

Fig. 6-3. *A typical built-in closet storage system for bedrooms. Moveable cabinets can increase the effective storage space (courtesy of White Home Products, Inc.).*

Some older homes sometimes have sewing rooms or other in-between-size rooms just off of the bedroom. In some cases, you might want to use this room for its intended purpose, that is, as a sewing room or other small work area. You might also want to renovate the room so it can be used as a large walk-in closet. For most buyers, the room will be more useful as a storage area instead of a work area.

Surface Considerations

Because bedrooms are personal rooms, you generally have more design options. You can do what you want to do when it comes to wall coverings, floor coverings, and window coverings.

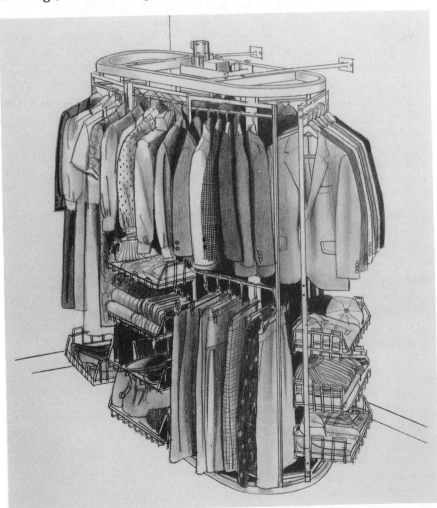

Fig. 6–4. *A moveable, carousel closet-storage system can help you fit a lot of storage into a small space (courtesy of White Home Products, Inc.).*

Many homeowners, for instance, decide to take advantage of unique *wallcoverings* such as rice paper, wooden slats, mirrored walls, fabric coverings, etc. This is fine, but don't make the mistake of using a covering that is too permanent. Removing mirrored panels that are glued to the wall, for instance, often require new owners to tear the sheetrock off down to the studs. Shoppers will see this as an expensive and messy process that will put a damper on their interest in your house. Paint or wallpaper are always safe coverings. Try to use neutral, light-colored hues so that the room appears as large as possible. When it comes to children's rooms, you can use brighter colors but select coverings that can be easily cleaned.

Rarely do bedrooms have *floor coverings* other than carpets or hardwood floors. If the bedroom has hardwood floors, it is highly recommended that you cover the floor with area rugs for a couple of reasons. For one thing, area rugs will deaden the noise when your house is shown to prospective buyers. A noisy bedroom will scare off buyers. Secondly, area rugs will add a sense of warmth to the room, making it more comfortable. In just about any climate, bare hardwood floors are cold in the mornings when your bare feet hit the floor. A covered floor will be more comfortable and add to energy efficiency. Always have as much floor covering as possible in children's rooms. Bare hardwood floors in the children's bedrooms will be scratched and dented and need to be protected as much as possible. Prospective home buyers do not want to have to deal with refinishing wooden floors because it is such an expensive and dirty job.

Window coverings in the bedroom serve several purposes. Not only do they provide privacy, they also help conserve energy, add to comfort, and play a big part in the aesthetics of a room. If a bedroom is unusually small, stay away from heavy fabric coverings; they will make the room appear smaller in size. As with the wall coverings, use light-colored, neutral colors. While miniblinds are attractive and provide privacy, they often do not add to the sense of warmth that many home sellers try to establish. Be careful before investing a lot of money into miniblinds for the bedroom.

REMODELING STRATEGIES

The bedroom is not the first room homeowners worry about remodeling after buying a house. Typically, more people remodel their bedrooms in the second or third year after buying a house, after the kitchen and bathroom. In master bedrooms that have enough size, major renovations often include adding a private bath and otherwise expanding the master suite concept (also discussed in this chapter). A contractor-installed bathroom addition to a bedroom usually costs between $3,500 and $7,000. It is generally considered to be worth the money, however, because you can recoup from 75 to 125 percent of that amount. If you do much of the work yourself, you can lower the cost to about $2,500 and recoup even more of your investment. In short, adding a bathroom to a bedroom is a safe investment.

Other renovations usually include adding access to an outdoor patio or deck. This involves installing atrium or sliding doors to the bedroom at a cost of about $1,000. Adding a deck or balcony to the outside of the bedroom might cost another $2,500. One advantage of remodeling a bedroom in this manner is that it often opens up a bare wall, making a small room seem much larger. You must consider energy efficiency (large expanses of glass windows can run up your heating or cooling bills) as well as security issues, however. If you are remodeling only for the investment value, you can put your money to better use elsewhere in the house. Adding a patio or deck will recoup no more than about 55 percent of your investment when selling the house.

If your house does not have enough bedrooms, you might want to add some more. While there are several ways to go about this, the most popular means are converting an existing attic or basement or adding an entire room to the house. Figure 6-5 shows a basement that was converted to a bedroom.

Fig. 6-5. *Basements can be converted into attractive bedrooms (courtesy of Armstrong World Industries, Inc.).*

Converting attics are one of the better remodeling investments you can make to a home, particularly if the renovation includes a bathroom. You can generally plan on spending about $10,000 to convert approximately 500 square feet of attic space to usable bedroom space. If you do all of the work yourself, you can complete the project for less than $5,000. In most cases, your return on investment will be almost 100 percent. Again, the more work you do yourself, the greater your return on investment. When you do the work yourself, that return can go up to as much as 150 percent.

Attic conversions are not as simple as they might appear at first glance. You cannot, for instance, simply begin laying flooring on top of your 2-×-4 ceiling joists because they aren't designed to support all of the additional weight that will be put on them. Instead, you will have to install 2-×-8 floor joists so that the additional weight does not rest on the ceiling below it. You must also be aware of building codes that govern stairs, ceiling heights, window, and other building aspects.

Adding a bedroom to the house is obviously more expensive than converting existing space, and you can plan on spending from $20,000 to $30,000 for a 500-square-foot room addition. The relatively high cost of this type of project makes it more difficult to recoup your investment. It might be worth the trouble and expense, however, if you plan on being in the house a long time before selling it.

Limited storage space is often enough reason to justify the adding or remodeling of a room. However, a simpler solution is *respacing*, which is really nothing more than making more efficient use of existing space. Traditional closet storage systems involved the old-fashioned plank-and-pole closet, which usually provides half the storage possible for available floor space. A 2-×-8-foot closet, for example, has 16 square feet of floor space, but a plank-and-pole closet provides only 8 feet of storage space. By employing more efficient respacing techniques, you should be able to get a full 16 feet of storage space. In fact, according to companies that provide respacing alternatives, respacing can add the equivalent of a 10-×-12-square-foot room to a typical three-bedroom home.

Respacing usually involves nothing more than building in factory-built storage systems that include the traditional hanging/storage shelf along with efficiently designed shelves, drawers, and hanging rods. Figures 6-6 and 6-7 illustrate a couple of such closets, while Table 6-1 describes typical amounts of storage space gained when respacing techniques are implemented.

BUYER PREFERENCE

Bedrooms used to be for sleeping. Because of this, their basic design was dictated by the shape of the bed, usually square or rectangular. The room was laid out in a simple boxlike fashion, with the bed being the focal point of the room. A window or two was usually present and a closet available for storage. A fancy bedroom might have an adjoining half-bath, often shared with another bedroom, while an extravagant bedroom might have a full-bath. One reason more attention hasn't been paid to the bedroom is that it is not a room that typically is in public view. Homeowners

Fig. 6-6. *A master bedroom with an efficiently designed, respaced closet (courtesy of Clairson International).*

Fig. 6-7. *A child's bedroom closet also can be respaced to allow for more storage space (courtesy of Clairson International).*

**Table 6-1. Estimated Amount of Storage
Space Gained When Closet Respacing is Used.**

Storage Area	Size	Traditional Plank-and-Pole Storage	Respaced Storage
Master bedroom closet	6-×-8 feet	18 feet	48 feet
Child's bedroom closet	2-×-8 feet	8 feet	16 feet
Linen closet	2-×-3 feet	15 feet (3 shelves)	25 feet (5 shelves)
Kitchen pantry	2-×-6 feet	24 feet (3 shelves)	40 feet (5 shelves)
Utility/ Laundry room	6-×-8 feet	18 feet	36 feet

find it an easy place to cut corners when it comes to room design and planning. Even with this somewhat, at least by today's standards, utilitarian design, people still spent about one-third of their time in the bedroom, though most of that time spent was asleep.

How Many Bedrooms?

In 1950, two out of three houses built had only two bedrooms. Today, only one out of four houses built are limited to two bedrooms, and one out of every five homes built have four or more bedrooms.

Construction figures such as these obviously reflect buyer preferences. Fewer than 10 percent of today's home shoppers indicate that they would even be interested in looking at a two-bedroom house, let alone seriously consider buying one. (As you may suspect, the number of buyers interested in one-bedroom units is even less.) Similarly, the number of buyers who want five or more bedrooms is about the same as the number who are satisfied with two bedrooms. In general, the more expensive the house, the more home buyers want to have additional bedrooms.

Even though today's smaller-sized family usually isn't large enough to utilize four bedrooms, home shoppers still consider three or four bedrooms the minimum requirement in an average house. The most important bedroom to buyers is the master suite, which is expected to be larger and more elaborate than other bedrooms in the house.

As for the other bedrooms, buyers want to use at least one of the secondary bedrooms for something other than sleeping. Typical uses include a home office, hobby area, exercise room, or simply a guest room. Because of personal computers, telecommuting, and other work-related activities, bedrooms need extra electrical outlets and telephone connectors. The implication for home designers is that secondary bedrooms should have adequate electrical, telephone, cable television, and other wiring capabilities to support these nontraditional activities.

How Big Should Bedrooms Be?

Cramped bedrooms are both uninviting and unattractive. Not only will you find them difficult to live in, but you will also discover that home shoppers will immediately take note of their size and usually express a negative reaction to that size.

Traditionally, the basic factor that determines the size of a bedroom has been the bed. A standard double bed takes up about 30 square feet of floor space, a king-size bed requires about 42 square feet. If the bed is the only thing you had to accommodate in a room, you could easily get by with floor space slightly greater than that of the bed. That isn't the case anymore because bedrooms provide much more than just sleeping quarters.

You also must consider the placement of the bed and the space around it. Place a bed so that there is at least 40 inches between the foot of the bed and the nearest wall, door, or piece of furniture. On the sides of the bed, allow at least 30 inches from the wall, another bed (if twin beds are used), or furniture. Master bedrooms that accommodate two people need at least one uninterrupted wall (no windows or doors) that is 10 feet long. For secondary bedrooms, that wall should be at least 8 feet in length.

Another way of looking at this is that, at a bare minimum, the room should be at least three times larger than the bed that is in it. The minimum size for a bedroom that will have a standard double bed should be about 100 square feet laid out as close to a square as possible, 10 × 10 feet or 8 × 12 feet for instance. A room with a king-size bed should be at least 125 square feet, say, 10 × 12 or 10 × 13 feet.

You also must look at other bedroom furniture when evaluating the size of the room. Most bedroom furniture, like night stands and dressers, is built to standard sizes in depth. This is important in terms of floor space and room size. Most furniture usually comes out from the wall between 18 inches and 24 inches. The length is much more variable. Keep in mind that all of these dimensions are considered minimum requirements.

THE MASTER SUITE

There's no question that the most important bedroom to home buyers is the master suite. As its name suggests, the master suite is much more than just a bedroom. Today's master suite usually includes a full-size bath, perhaps a personal relaxation area, sometimes a spa or sauna, and even a personal home-entertainment center. Because of features such as these, the prevailing attitude among homeowners is that bedrooms aren't just for nighttime sleeping, and they are consequently spending more time during daylight hours in the master suite. It is easy to understand why the master suite is beginning to be known as a "home within a home."

One reason buyers place so much emphasis on the master suite is that it is the one room in the house that individuals don't have to share with others. It is a personal room, not a public room. The layout, design, furnishing, and colors can therefore be more personal than anywhere else in the house.

The specific location of the master bedroom is more important to home buyers than the location of secondary bedrooms. By far, most home buyers want the master bedroom situated on the rear of the house. This holds true for both single-story and two-story houses. If you are designing your own home, locate the master suite first, then worry about fitting the secondary bedrooms in later. A surprising number of home shoppers also indicate that they want the master suite located separate from the secondary bedrooms.

Even though the master suites tend to be larger than other bedrooms, space consideration is still of prime importance. Buyers obviously want an uncramped sleeping area, which means larger than the minimum dimensions. They also want the master suite to have walk-in closets, a sitting area, and a large bath. Clearly, large baths and greater than average storage space are considered the most because three-quarters of all home shoppers want a private bath in the master suite and walk-in closets. Of far less importance in terms of need and space requirements to home shoppers are dressing/makeup areas and balconies or patios. What is important to remember is that when space trade-offs need to be made, a large closet and small sitting area is more important than small closets and a large dressing area. If you are faced with an instance of low-storage area, you'd be well advised to make the most of the available space, however limited. (See the earlier discussion in this chapter regarding closet respacing for techniques on making the most efficient use of storage space.)

When it comes to the bathing area of the master suite, home shoppers generally prefer baths with separate tub and showers as opposed to simply a stall shower or a shower/tub combination. There is no real preference for raised tubs over sunken ones, but there is a decided preference for oversized tubs. Buyers also have expressed a preference for baths that are made up of several smaller rooms, (or compartments) instead of a single large room containing the tub, shower, toilet, and vanity. This lets a couple use the facilities at the same time (one person can shave while the other baths, for instance), yet still have the privacy provided by a private bathroom.

As with those bathrooms not associated with the master suite, buyers consider durable, waterproof countertops made from Corian or ceramic tile to be especially desirable. They have also indicated that dual-basin vanities are important.

7

Living Rooms and Group- Activity Areas

Group-Activity Rooms like the living room, dining room, family room, and den present a unique problem for homeowners. They are some of the easiest rooms to design because they are open and flexible. At the same time, this same openness and flexibility also makes them difficult to design.

Size is a fundamental consideration for living and similar rooms that are intended for group activities such as entertaining, reading, eating, playing games, studying, watching television, etc. The rooms must be large enough to hold enough furniture to seat groups of people comfortably, but flexible enough that the furniture can be moved around for large or small groups of people.

Even though living rooms and family rooms have similar functions, they have very different layouts and designs. Most homeowners prefer to have the family room, which is generally less formal than a living room, located near the kitchen and near an outside entrance, usually to the backyard. Because the living room is used primarily for entertaining guests, it is better to locate it near the front entrance so that guests do not have to walk through the entire house to reach the room.

When it comes to showing the house to prospective buyers, the two types of rooms also serve different functions. The living room should impress buyers with its size and elegance. Because the living room is usually near the front of the house, it is often the first room the buyer sees and, consequently, plays a big part in providing the initial impression the buyer has of your house. The family room, however, should relax the buyer. It should be a room where family members can kick back their heels, listen to music, watch television, or take it easy. Together, the two rooms tell home buyers a lot about you and the house you are selling.

DESIGN STRATEGIES

All group-activity rooms must somehow effectively provide a balance between traffic zones and sitting areas. This is not always an easy task for designers or architects. In a family room, for instance, one person might be trying to watch television, while other family members might be going in and out of the house or back and forth from the kitchen. If the room is not laid out effectively, then the two incompatible activities will result in tension instead of relaxation.

Accordingly, when looking at a group-activity room, first identify the sitting areas, then the traffic areas. Sitting areas can be fixed locations designated by fireplaces, windows, or other such room features. Traffic zones are usually designated by doorways that go into and out of a room. Hopefully, the shortest path from one doorway to the other will not pass directly through a sitting area. If so, you might want to consider remodeling the room, closing off the doorway, or other available options because the room won't produce the effect you are striving for.

Keep in mind that family rooms in particular will be used by all family members, young and old. If you regularly need space for solitude and privacy, consider a den. Don't try for total solitude and privacy in a family or living room.

FIREPLACES

One feature that is often common to all sorts of group-activity rooms is a fireplace. Pay special attention to the fireplace because of its importance to home buyers. In just about every survey conducted by real estate companies, fireplaces rate as the one house feature that shoppers look for. In most cases, more than three out of every four home shoppers indicate that fireplaces play an important part in their buying decisions.

Part of the reason for this is that, whether they are used on a regular basis or not, fireplaces are aesthetically pleasing. The bricks or stones from which the fireplace is built often break up a long wall or empty corner, and the mantle provides an ideal place to show off clocks, vases, or other attractive accessories. Furthermore, fireplaces bring people together simply because it is natural to position chairs in a semicircle around the hearth, Fig. 7-1.

Fireplaces can go in just about any room in the house—family rooms, living rooms, bedrooms, and even kitchens—and many homes now have more than one fireplace. When a house can have only one fireplace, however, about two out of every three home shoppers say that they would prefer to have it in the family room instead of the living room. At the same time, about one out of every four shoppers indicated that they would like to have a fireplace in the master suite.

When showing your house to prospective buyers in the winter, the fireplace lets you add both a literal and symbolic sense of warmth to the house if you have a fire going. In the summer, it is better to keep the fireplace clean and simply have logs stacked in the firebox.

LIVING ROOMS

If you've done any home decorating at all, you probably already know that homeowners spend more money decorating and furnishing the living

Fig. 7-1. *A fireplace, like the one in this family room, makes a natural sitting area that brings people together (courtesy of Armstrong World Industries, Inc.).*

room than any other room in the house. Nevertheless, there are a few basic features that make living rooms particularly attractive to home shoppers—size, quality, and, as already discussed, a fireplace.

There are several qualities about the living room that should be obvious to the home shopper. For one thing, the living room should convey a sense of cordiality, warmth, and grace. This ambience is achieved by making use of broad views, both inside the room and through windows to the outside. High, cathedral ceilings help impart this feeling as do hardwood floors and built-in cabinets and bookcases.

In many houses, the front door opens directly into the living room. If you have any say in the design or layout of the house, try to avoid this situation. Instead, design a small entryway or hallway to provide transition space for visitors as they enter the house. Not only will you find this layout more convenient, but home buyers will also respond favorably. Nearly three out of every four buyers, in fact, say that they prefer a transitional entryway into the house instead of having the door open directly into the living room. In cold or wet climates, this provides family members and visitors a place to remove wet coats and footgear. Consequently, the entryway probably should have a small coat closet and a waterproof, easy-to-clean floor covering—ceramic or natural stone, for instance, or even vinyl tile.

If at all possible, make the entryway as dramatic as you can and have it convey the impression of space. This can be done by having a room that steps up or down from the foyer. Having a vestibule that provides a direct view of the outside, perhaps at the end of a hallway, is also very effective. In larger homes, the sense of space can be enhanced by using high-volume ceilings or two-story windows. In smaller houses, a simple rail might suffice.

Many of today's living rooms are referred to as a *great room* because the open layout, which often takes in the living and dining room, provides the single greatest amount of unbroken floor space in the house. While a layout such as this is flexible, it does present some space problems if furniture isn't efficiently positioned. The great room in Fig. 7-2, for instance, is laid out so that two separate conversation areas can be accommodated in a single room.

Solid-colored, neutral wallcoverings are usually preferred in living rooms because of the large wall space. Large expanses of patterned wallpapers make the room look busy, and dark colors make it look small.

More important than living room walls, however, are the room's floors. Virtually every home shopper considers the living room floor a key element. It is usually the first thing the shopper sees when he or she enters the room. A scratched or stained floor will, in the buyer's mind, decrease the value of the house. If your living room has a wood floor (hardwood, parquet, etc.), it is worth your time and effort to see that it is in good or excellent condition. Home buyer's will likewise perceive stained or worn wall-to-wall carpeting as a negative factor. Have carpets cleaned or replaced before showing the house to buyers.

Use your windows and window coverings in the living room to show off the room. Don't fall into the trap of providing too many windows in the living room, however, especially too many windows that are quite large. For one thing, buyer's immediately see windows, particularly living room windows, as a high-maintenance feature (that is, they need to be washed a lot), and many of today's home buyer's are looking specifically for low-maintenance homes. Today's homeowner also values privacy; consequently, large windows in the living room are often covered with drapes to ensure this privacy. Large windows also pose security problems—they allow burglars to either see what you have in the room or gain entry into the house.

Fig. 7-2. *A large living room can be efficiently laid out so that space potential is maximized (courtesy of Armstrong World Industries, Inc.).*

Home buyers who are concerned about energy efficiency might be concerned about rooms that have large glass windows because the glass requires special insulation in extremely cold or hot weather. Finally, many buyer's know that drapery or blinds for large windows can cost hundreds of dollars to replace and that they must be cleaned every year or so. Too many windows present decorating problems because there might not be enough room for attractive wallhangings (photos, paintings, etc.). With all of this in mind, living room windows still enable you to showcase your house and are certainly preferable to rooms with too few windows.

Special lighting is commonly used more in the living room than any other room in the house. Windows let you take advantage of natural light during daylight hours. By using light colors and mirrors in the living room, you can further make the most of sunlight. At night, spotlights, floor lamps, accent lighting, and other focused, but subdued, lighting can be used to show off the room. If at all possible, be sure that the living room has plenty of electrical outlets along the walls so that lights can be placed as strategically as possible. Do not rely on bright ceiling lights, especially when you are showing the house to buyers.

DINING ROOMS

The dining room is different from other group-activity rooms because it is designed for a specific function, eating. With this function in mind, two things are important when it comes to laying out the space for a dining room—location and size.

It is very important to locate the dining room next to the kitchen, Fig. 7-3. Furthermore, centrally locate the dining room between the food preparation area and entertainment areas like the living room. This will make the room convenient for both guests and family members. If the house is designed around an open great room, the dining room can actually be in the same area as the living room with no doors separating the two areas.

Because dining rooms often require large dining tables and accompanying chairs as well as hutches and side tables, having adequate space is also important. Dining rooms that are too small to accommodate a dining table of even moderate size often causes more problems than it solves because it can make entertaining an uncomfortable event.

In many of today's homes, formal dining rooms that have traditionally been used only for holidays or other special events might as well be on an endangered species list because homeowners tend to prefer large, open, great rooms. That doesn't mean that you can forget about the dining room altogether. It is important that there be somewhere, other than the kitchen table or snack bar, for guests to be entertained and fed and for special meals or events to take place. While you might not want to have a complete set of formal dining room furniture, you should at least have room and enough flexibility to provide for more formal events.

FAMILY ROOMS

Informal family rooms have undergone a dramatic change over the last two decades. Thirty years ago, family rooms generally didn't exist, although some houses had paneled basements that doubled as "rec" rooms.

About twenty years ago, informal group-activity rooms became more important to homeowners, but they were still a luxury enjoyed by only a few families. Although remodeled basements continued to be the most common family room, many homeowners undertook more elaborate projects by actually adding family rooms to the house. These rooms usually included a fireplace and sliding patio doors that encouraged informal traffic and activities.

Fortunately, the prevailing attitude today's homeowners have towards informal group-activity rooms is that they are integral parts of the

Fig. 7-3. *Locate dining rooms near the kitchen (courtesy of Armstrong World Industries, Inc.).*

house. Family rooms that are separate from formal living rooms are considered very important to a house, especially for families with small children who need to be watched. Consequently, family rooms have been moved out of the basement to the mainstream of the house.

More than anything else, design and decorate your family room so that it is comfortable, relaxing, and enjoyable. To help convey this sense, many family rooms have a rustic decor—unpainted brick or stone fireplaces, paneled walls, etc. Because children might frequently come into the family room from outside, and all family members might occasionally eat in the room, it is also a good idea to use neutral or dark-colored carpets. These won't show stains as easily as carpets used in a more formal room.

Size is important when it comes to family rooms. Keep in mind that these rooms are designed for a group of people, not just one or two

Fig. 7-4. *Having the family room located next to the kitchen is very important, especially to home buyers who have small children (courtesy of Armstrong World Industries, Inc.).*

126

individuals seeking privacy. Family members will gather in the family room to watch television, play games, or simply converse. The room must therefore be large enough for group-activity furnishings—a television, card table, sofa, piano, whatever.

Two fundamental design principles govern family rooms. The most important basic element is that family rooms, like the one in Fig. 7-4, are located next to the kitchen. This enables adults, who spend a lot of time in the kitchen, to easily monitor the activities of small children without having to run up and down stairs or go from one end of the house to the other. Having an informal room next to the kitchen also makes it easy to entertain or enjoy leisurely snacks or meals while watching television or other such activities. In many houses, all that separates the family room from the kitchen is a countertop; this is a design that is not only convenient but one that opens up both rooms.

The second important element is to locate family rooms near an outdoor entrance, usually to the backyard or patio. This is convenient for families who like to entertain or eat outside and for children who can play inside and out. Having an outside door is especially convenient for those family rooms that have a fireplace. Firewood won't have to be carried through the entire house on the way in, and then, ashes won't have to be carried through on the way out.

There are several design features in a family room that home shoppers look for, the most important being a fireplace. Home buyers like the sense of coziness that a fireplace adds to a room, particularly to a room that will be used for casual, homey group get-togethers. Make good use of doors that have large expanses of glass (sliding or atrium doors, for instance) and large windows that open up the room and make it appear larger.

DENS

At one time, dens and family rooms were considered pretty much the same, and the difference between them was really nothing more than a matter of semantics. Both were informal areas designed for group activities, and few houses, if any, had a family room and a den. Over the years, however, the definition of the two rooms has gravitated towards extremes. Family rooms have become associated with group activities, while dens now tend to provide more privacy. In houses that have both a family room and a den, the den is where someone might go to get away from the television noise in the family room. Dens have also become the center for home offices, Fig. 7-5.

While group-oriented family rooms are now considered integral to the design of a house, dens are still thought to be nonessential. Few homes are built with a specific room designated as the den. Instead, homeowners try to provide at least one flexible room that can serve as a den, office, or extra bedroom if necessary. More often than not, this room is located on the ground floor, if the house has more than one floor. If the den is to be used as a home office and if clients or other business associates will be calling, it might also be convenient to have that room near a front entrance of the house, or perhaps a side door instead of the main entrance. It is also probably a good idea to locate the room near a bathroom or powder room for the convenience of business-related callers.

Unlike family rooms that lean towards an open design, dens tend to be more private. Because a den might occasionally be used as a guest bedroom, you might want to build a Murphy bed into the wall or use a hide-a-bed sofa in the room. Because the den might not be subjected to heavy traffic, it can also accommodate more storage—closets, shelves, etc.—than the family room.

REMODELING STRATEGIES

Remodeling a house to accommodate group-activity rooms can vary from a minor upgrade of existing space to the major job of adding a single

Fig. 7-5. *Dens are often turned into home offices (courtesy of Armstrong World Industries, Inc.).*

room or entire wing to a house. Obviously, the cost of the remodeling job will depend upon the extent of the changes made to the original house.

Adding a fireplace to an existing living or family room is usually a good investment even in cases where one of the rooms (the living room, for instance) already has a fireplace. A working fireplace is valuable as an alternate source of heat if you use it on a regular basis and if firewood is relatively cheap. It is also a good emergency heating source during power outages.

If you decide to have a full-size brick or stone fireplace built, be aware that it needs a special foundation or other support. You can't simply build a real fireplace onto a floor, even if it is a slab-concrete floor, because a fireplace literally weighs thousands of pounds. There are other options available, however. Prefab fireplaces that can be built into the wall are generally much lighter in weight than masonry units and can be put up much quicker. Instead of brick or stone chimneys, for instance, they usually have metal flues. Likewise, the hearths might not be full-size brick or stone; instead, thin slices of brick that are mounted on sheets of backing are pasted onto the heat-resistant drywall. Finally, free-standing fireplaces are also available. While these are probably preferable to no fireplace at all, they really don't add much to the resale value of the house.

Usually, it costs about $3,000 to add a fireplace to an existing house. Because a quality fireplace often adds as much as $4,000 to the value of a house, fireplace additions are generally viewed as a good investment. Because fireplaces are potentially so dangerous, it is a good idea to have an expert build them unless you are an experienced do-it-yourselfer. A fireplace that you build yourself can cost much less, however, generally less than $1,500, yet still add two or three times that to the value of the house.

Converting a basement to a family room (Fig. 7-6) usually involves installing a ceiling (most commonly, a suspended ceiling), tiling or carpeting the floor, and paneling the walls. Associated tasks include wiring for light fixtures and outlets as well as installing doors into other areas of the basement. Home shoppers place much less value on remodeled basements than they once did, and even though it is a relatively inexpensive project, it won't add much value to the house. Consequently, you should try to keep your investment to a minimum, doing as much of the work yourself as possible. This should enable you to keep the cost to less than $2,000, and you'll probably recoup as much as 90 percent of your investment. Having someone else do the job for you sometimes costs as much as $6,000, and at this rate, you'll get back only about one-third of what you put into it.

As you might expect, adding a room to the house is a major project that can be very expensive. On average, you can plan on spending at least $20,000 to $30,000 to have a 500-square-foot room added onto your house. This figure includes such elements as foundation, walls, roof, roofing, insulation, wiring, and so on. Considering the high cost of this remodeling project, remember that your chances of recouping your investment increases the more work you do yourself. If you do everything yourself, your return can be as much as 150 percent of what you put in. If you have someone else do all the work for you, the return averages about 50 percent. In general, a room addition is a good investment, as long as you don't spend too much money.

There are many variables that affect the total cost—the quality of the materials, the cost of labor in your area, whether or not you do any of the work yourself—but plan on spending at least the minimum amount on any room addition. If you want to add features like fireplaces or atrium doors, the cost will increase.

While the size of the room addition is directly related to the cost of the project, some homeowners are surprised to learn that square footage is less of a determining factor than they thought. Doubling the size of

Fig. 7-6. *Drab basements can be renovated into attractive and functional family rooms (courtesy of Armstrong World Industries, Inc.).*

a room addition, for instance, won't necessarily double the cost of the project. In the same sense, halving the size won't cut the cost in half either.

BUYER PREFERENCE

Home shoppers naturally assume that every house will have a living room. Increasingly, however, shoppers are beginning to expect that other group-activity rooms—formal dining rooms and informal family rooms—be included in the home design.

Because the living room is designed for formal entertaining where guests aren't expected to have free access to the house, three out of every four homeowners prefer to have the living room located at the front of the house. Buyers also prefer having a separate entry hall with a masonry floor into the house so that guests do not have to enter directly into the living room. Other preferred living room features include a fireplace and bay windows.

Fireplaces are the number one most desirable feature in a house. When a house can have only one fireplace, however, nearly three out of four buyers indicate that they prefer the fireplace be in the family room instead of the living room.

Family rooms themselves also rank high in buyer preference, right behind fireplaces and large kitchens. In addition to a fireplace, home shoppers want the family room to be as large as possible, even if it means a smaller living room and dining room. Because most buyers prefer that the family room be adjacent to the kitchen, two out of three home buyers want the family room at the rear of the house. While buyers do have a preference regarding the location of the living and family rooms, they do not really care where the dining room is located (that is, in the front or back of the house) as long as it is convenient to the kitchen.

8

Exterior Finish

Up to now, this book has largely focused on two points: the overall layout of a house and the features used inside it. The details home shoppers first notice about a house aren't necessarily floor plans or interior features. What they see before anything else is the exterior of the house—the color, siding, style, roofing, and so on. It is therefore imperative that you take whatever steps you can to showcase the outside of your house. It might be the only chance you get to present the house to a great number of potential buyers.

Although some features, such as the color of the siding, might be more predominant than others, the exterior appearance of a house is not defined by a single factor alone. Rather, it is a number of elements—color and type of roofing, style of windows, siding material—that work together to create an overall impression.

SIDING STRATEGIES

Without a doubt, exterior siding is the most dominant characteristic of the home's exterior. The most commonly used sidings include wood, stucco, masonry (brick, stone, etc.), vinyl, and aluminum. The type of siding used on a house depends upon a number of elements—geographical location, climatic conditions, house style, neighborhood characteristics, and owner preferences.

Many houses end up using a combination of different siding, like the one in Fig. 8-1. In most cases, this is fine, but it really isn't a good idea to use more than two siding materials on a single house or it begins to look busy.

Wood Siding

Not only is wood one of the most commonly used siding materials, it is also perhaps one of the most versatile of all the possible alternatives. One reason for this is that wood siding comes in many different forms, ranging from solid plank to manufactured hardboard. Moreover, it is available in both horizontal and vertical orientations as well as numerous styles (beveled, shiplap, board and batten, etc.).

Just about any kind of wood can be used for solid wood siding, although most species of wood must be protected by a coat of paint. Others,

Fig. 8-1. *Example of a house that uses a variety of siding materials. In this case, both brick and horizontally oriented wood siding is used (courtesy of Miles Homes, Inc.).*

such as cedar or redwood, can be left unpainted, although they will probably require some sort of preservative or water-resistant treatment. If your house has been painted on the outside, a fresh coat of paint will go a long way towards creating an initial positive impression on potential buyers.

The type of wood siding used on a house depends on the style of house it is, the style of the other homes in the neighborhood, and your own personal preferences. Rarely will you see a large colonial home with large expanses of vertical wood siding; that style just isn't conducive to vertical lines. Vertical siding, however, can be very attractive in smaller homes, like the one in Fig. 8-2. Because it is economical and relatively quick to install, *plywood siding* is being used on more and more of today's houses. *Manufactured hardboard siding* is also relatively inexpensive to install, and it has the added benefit of not being prone to splitting or cracking as natural wood sometimes does.

Cedar shingles are often used as siding on houses, particularly those that have a rustic appeal to them. Even though they are durable, wooden siding shingles are both time-consuming and expensive to apply, and

Fig. 8-2. *Vertical wood siding is particularly attractive on smaller homes (courtesy of Miles Homes, Inc.).*

they require the same water-repellent protection as any other natural wood siding. On the plus side, cedar shakes and shingles come in a variety of attractive styles, as Fig. 8-3 shows.

With all this in mind, the most commonly applied wood siding is still *horizontal solid clapboard with beveled edges*. This siding comes in varying widths and thickness and, because of its traditional look, appeals to many home shoppers. As the house in Fig. 8-4 illustrates, it can be used with a variety of homes.

Brick, Masonry, and Stucco Siding

Masonry wallcoverings such as brick, stucco, and stone have long been one of the siding materials most preferred by home shoppers. That's the good news, if you are selling a home that already has brick or stone siding. The bad news is that masonry-based sidings also cost more than other alternatives because of the additional time, trouble, and effort required to apply them to the house. Nevertheless, if you are in the planning stages of building a house, it is to your long-term advantage to use these siding materials if you want them.

Houses with *brick siding* in particular are in demand by shoppers. One reason for this is that, especially when the siding is unpainted, the house tends to require less maintenance than comparable houses that have other types of siding. (Trim around windows and under eaves still requires maintenance on a regular basis, however.) Don't forget that all bricks aren't alike and that all brick homes don't end up looking alike either. Not only do bricks come in different colors, but they are available with different finishes and different shades.

Another attractive, yet durable, siding is *stone*. Just as wood siding is available in a variety of species, several different types of stone siding are available too. Cut sandstone or other stones that come from a quarry make nice facings and are almost as easy to put up as brick. It takes more time, effort, and money, however, to apply exterior siding using unevenly shaped fieldstones. Even though many people find fieldstone an attractive siding material, the difficulty of working with it has made it impractical for builders except in cases where custom homes are being built.

Stucco is different from brick and stones in that it is plastered onto the sides of houses instead of laid. Because stucco is relatively easy to install and it conveys much of the sense of permanence enjoyed by brick or stone, it is a popular siding material in many parts of the country. Furthermore, it is easy to paint and stands up well over the years.

Vinyl and Aluminum Siding

There's a lot to be said for both *vinyl* and *aluminum siding*. They are durable, inexpensive, require little maintenance, and are relatively easy to install. Both are available in a variety of colors and patterns and have optional insulation that helps keep a cold house warm.

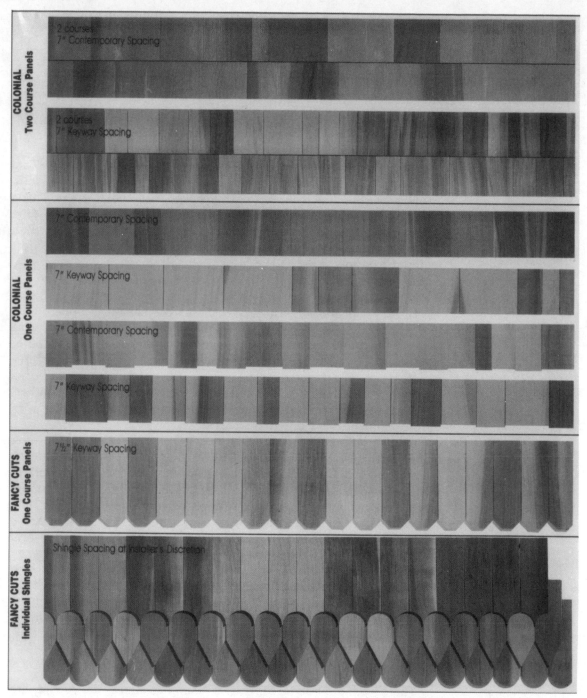

Fig. 8-3. *Cedar shingles come in a variety of styles (courtesy of Shakertown Siding).*

With all of these pluses, it is surprising that more homeowners don't choose either siding option. That's generally the case, however. Part of the basis for homeowner's dislike of aluminum and vinyl might be the connotation of cheapness associated with lightweight materials like plastic and aluminum. Both materials are also relatively noisy and are more easily damaged than, say, brick. A stone thrown by a lawnmower, for instance, can puncture vinyl siding or dent aluminum.

Vinyl and aluminum siding can be attractive features to empty nesters or single home shoppers who are particularly interested in low-maintenance homes. Furthermore, vinyl and aluminum can effectively be used in conjunction with brick or other siding, especially if the vinyl/aluminum is used in hard-to-paint areas below the eaves.

Composite or Hardboard Siding

An alternative to the sometimes "manufactured" look of vinyl/aluminum siding and the upkeep and cost of natural (wood and brick) siding is a fabricated *composite*, or hardboard, siding. This siding typically

Fig. 8-4. *Traditional horizontal wood siding looks good on just about any house (courtesy of Miles Homes, Inc.).*

consists of Masonite or of wood chips that are formed into panels under heat and pressure. Such siding has the advantage of natural wood in that it does not have the imperfections of knots and sap discoloration, nor does it tend to check or split. Unlike aluminum or vinyl, hardboard siding does require painting. On the other hand, composite siding tends to be less noisy than those materials, particularly when heavy hail, rain, or wind is pelting the house. Like vinyl and aluminum, some hardboard sidings come prefinished from the factory and do not need to be painted for 5 to 25 years.

Composite siding is a relatively inexpensive, durable, and lightweight siding material. It comes in a variety of embossed textures that more closely resemble natural wood than do vinyl or aluminum. Composite siding, which comes in a variety of styles from simulated cedar to simulated stucco (Fig. 8-5), is considered a viable option, particularly for do-it-yourself remodelers since it can be installed relatively easily (it usually comes in 4-×-8 sheets) and at a generally lower cost than other siding options.

ROOF STRATEGIES

The roof is one of those things that, if it is done right, you never notice. If the roof isn't done correctly, however, it stands out like a proverbial sore thumb. Unobtrusive roofs are achieved by giving careful thought to colors, materials, and patterns that fit into the all-around exterior scheme of the house.

There are other factors to consider when selecting a roof. Many areas have building codes and fire regulations that prohibit the use of some

Fig. 8-5. *Composite sidings are manufactured to simulate a variety of common siding alternatives (courtesy of Cladwood, a division of Smurfit Newsprint Corp.).*

roofing materials, particularly wooden shakes or shingles. It would be a mistake to install untreated shakes without first getting clearance from the proper authorities, especially in dry climates. Likewise, many buyers have been scared by horror stories surrounding wooden roofs and are leery of houses that have them.

Although energy conservation isn't a prime concern of home buyers anymore, common sense and the desire for comfort dictate that houses in hot climates should have light-colored roofs so that the sunlight is reflected. Conversely, homes in cold climates should have dark-colored roofs that absorb as much of the sun's warmth as possible.

When buying a home, the last thing most home buyers want to worry about is having to deal with a big (and expensive) job like replacing the roof in the near future. If you find yourself in the position of having to replace the roof before selling it, it is a good idea to choose a high-quality, long-lasting roofing material. Unlike a cheap paint job, a cheap roof will turn buyers away. The roof is not a place to cut corners.

Composite Shingles

The most common type of roofing shingles are often grouped together under the classification of composite shingles and include both asphalt and fiberglass materials. They are generally the easiest and least expensive shingles to install on a roof. They come in a wide variety of colors and a few different patterns.

Different grades of composite shingles are available, ranging from those that last 10 years to those that last up to 40 years. While it might not be necessary for you to have the 40-year shingles installed (remember that the typical family only lives in a particular house an average of 7 years), you should definitely avoid those roofing materials that are only good for up to 10 years. Shingles that are guaranteed from 20 to 30 years will more than serve your purposes and impress a shopper.

Wood Shingles and Shakes

Perhaps the most attractive roofing materials are wooden shingles and shakes. As mentioned before, however, they are also the most dangerous because as they dry out, they can catch fire very easily. For this reason alone, home shoppers have become wary of wooden roofs. Fire-resistant treatments are available for wood roofs, and if your house has been so treated, be sure to use it as a selling point when showing the house to prospective buyers. Only about one in ten buyers say they would try to save money by selecting untreated shakes over fire-resistant treated shakes.

Wood shingles go well with many different types of house, from contemporary to log homes. If you are willing to pay the higher installation price and are prepared to deal with the fire-resistant issues surrounding them, wood shingles are a viable option.

Metal Shingles

At one time, *copper roofs* were considered one of the prime roofing materials. More recently, the price of the metal has made copper an impractical roofing material, except in rare instances. While copper roofs are occasionally used in higher priced homes, aluminum roofing materials have become much more accepted.

Although still relatively expensive when compared to composite shingles, *aluminum shingles* are extremely durable and are gaining in popularity, especially with homeowners who are interested in low maintenance. If there is a drawback to aluminum shingles it is that some have a glossy finish that reflects light and detracts from the subtlety of the roof.

Clay or Concrete Tile Shingles

Clay and concrete tile shingles create very attractive roofs but require extensive support because of their great weight. This also adds to the cost, which is already greater than other types of roofs in the first place because of the higher cost of materials and labor. As the house in Fig. 8-6

Fig. 8-6. *Clay tile makes an attractive and durable roofing option (courtesy of the Fieldstone Co.).*

illustrates, slate and clay can produce handsome roofs that can last longer than any roofing material. Surveys indicate, however, that most buyers are willing to pay the extra money to have clay tile roofs, particularly in warm climates where clay tiles provide better cooling.

COLOR STRATEGIES

When it comes to presenting the exterior of your house to possible buyers, the single most important factor is the color scheme of the outside of the house. Just as important as the particular color of the siding is the way in which that color is coordinated with the rest of the exterior, specifically the color of trim (windows, doors, eaves, guttering, etc.) and the color of the roof.

Although many people have strong negative feelings about neutral colors they consider tiresome—colors like white, beige, gray, and tan— such colors appeal to a much wider cross section of home shoppers than bright, vivid colors. When coordinated with the color of the roof and the trim, neutral colors help create a sense of warmth and hominess in the mind of the buyer.

Owners of small houses in particular should be careful about the choice of colors. The application of relatively large, unbroken expanses of light, neutral colors can make a small house appear larger than it would appear if it were painted with bright or dark colors. Keep in mind that the effect of a neutral siding color can be counteracted by dark or bright trim that breaks up the light-colored walls. Consequently, it is important that neutral, but compatible, colors be used on both the siding and trim.

From the point of view of energy conservation, light roofs tend to be preferable in hot climates, and dark roofs are better in cold climates. If your house has a complicated roof profile, however, a darker color might tend to unify the various planes better than a light-colored roof. This doesn't necessarily mean that black should be used; there are dark or semidark colors that can be coordinated with the color of the siding.

Finally, don't forget the houses around you. While you don't necessarily have to make your house look like every other house on the block, you don't want it to stand out too much either. Neutral colors will help you achieve this balance with neighboring homes.

So what colors are appropriate for houses that might be up for sale before long? Stick with siding that is painted white, beige, tan, light brown, putty, sand, colonial blue, gray, or shades of each. Select appropriate colors for the trim; white for gray and colonial blue; putty or brown for tan, beige, or putty; and so on. Check at your local paint store and ask for neutral, yet coordinated, colors.

DOORS

As was mentioned previously, it is very important—for resale purposes—for you to have a dramatic front door and entryway, like the doors shown in Fig. 8-7. One reason is that the first thing buyers will notice when approaching the house is the front door. In addition to considering the attractiveness of a door, you must also consider both security and energy efficiency. The importance of attractive and safe doors applies to all exterior doors in the house, including doors to decks and patios (Fig. 8-8), as well as the front door.

Entrances for people aren't the only doors in the house to be mindful of, however. Garage doors are also important to consider. When garages were relegated to back alleys, it generally wasn't important what they

Fig. 8-7. *To maximize the resale value of a house, the front door should be as dramatic as possible, yet still provide security and energy efficiency (courtesy of Visador Co.).*

142

looked like, but those days are long gone. Now that most garage entrances are visible from the street, having an attractive and efficient garage door is very important to buyers for both cosmetic and security reasons.

Because garage doors are usually very large and heavy, modern garage doors are increasingly being made from lightweight, strong synthetic materials. Such doors don't split or crack like wood, they don't dent or bend like metal, and they don't come apart like plywood.

When home buyers mention garage-door features, however, from one-half to two-thirds of all shoppers expressly state that they would be

Fig. 8-7. *(Continued from page 142.)*

willing to pay extra for a garage-door opener. At a cost of only about $300 for installation, this is a worthwhile home improvement.

WINDOWS

Windows are another house component that are dealt with only as an afterthought. This is too bad because windows serve several significant roles in the house. For one thing, they provide the inside of the house with a source of natural light and, in cold weather, solar warmth. Windows also let fresh air into the house. Finally, and more relevant, windows play an important part in the exterior appearance of your house.

On the negative side, windows are often considered a high-maintenance item in the house because dirt, smears, raindrops, and other forms of grime show up so easily. Contrary to their passive solar heating benefits, windows also allow unwanted heat into the house during warm weather and let desired heat escape in cold weather. Windows also provide a security risk for the house because they are an easy means of

Fig. 8-8. *When providing attractive doors, don't forget about patio and other indoor/outdoor entrances as well (courtesy of Visador Co.).*

illegal entry. With all of these good and bad points, it is important that you pay attention to the size, style, and location of windows in your house.

There are several different types of windows available to homeowners, ranging from double-hung windows that slide up and down to ceiling windows that open onto the roof. There is no real "right" window for a house. The choice of window depends on the style of house, the climate, and the owner's particular preference.

What is more important to buyers than the style is the insulating value of a window. Home shoppers generally place more value on how well a window insulates a house than what that window looks like. Some areas have strict building codes that govern what kinds of windows are used. Double-paned insulating windows are almost always used in moderate to extreme climatic regions, while triple-pane glass might be required in extremely hot or cold parts of the country. Rarely are single-paned windows installed anymore, unless the plan calls for separate storm windows to be added later.

Another thing about windows that home shoppers tend to pay a lot of attention to is the type of frame. Wooden frames that are often used with traditional double-hung windows are a maintenance problem, something that you've discovered if you've ever had to paint trim every other year or so. For this reason, many homeowners have turned to aluminum frames, although they aren't as attractive and conduct more cold into the house. A better solution is to use vinyl-coated wooden frames with double-pane glass. Although this type of window is only available in a few selected colors and is relatively expensive, it is attractive and doesn't require the upkeep and maintenance of the other alternatives.

REMODELING STRATEGIES

The exterior of the house provides a real opportunity to easily and relatively inexpensively exhibit your home to shoppers. One of the first things you can do is apply a fresh coat of paint, something that shouldn't cost more than a couple of hundred dollars if you do it yourself. The eventual return, however, can be as much as 10 times that. Don't forget to scrape away any loose or flaking paint before applying a new coat, particularly on the trim. One tool that makes the job easier is a high-pressure water sprayer (gasoline or electric) that can be rented on a daily basis from just about any rental agency or paint store.

Professional painters will often charge as much as $2,000 or $3,000 to repaint a house. If you pay this much, be sure they use top-quality materials and that they properly prepare the siding and trim prior to painting. Within reason, whatever effort and expense you spend on exterior painting will pay off when you sell the house.

If your house has siding that is in extremely poor condition, you might consider installing new siding. Replacing existing wood siding with new materials can cost as much as $5,000 and require a contractor or carpenter. Again, this might be worth the expense and effort if the siding is broken or decayed. Installing vinyl or aluminum siding is an alternative and usually less expensive. Unless a buyer is specifically looking for a low-maintenance house, however, these forms of siding might not appeal to many home shoppers.

Cracks often appear in exterior stucco walls. Be sure to fill the cracks and apply paint when appropriate.

If your house has brick siding, repair all loose bricks and mortar. Considering the high cost involved in putting up brick siding, it isn't a good idea to install brick siding just to increase the resale value.

As was mentioned earlier, the roof is a crucial element when it comes to selling the home. Many selling contracts, in fact, require roof inspections and have contingency clauses to let the buyer out of the deal if it turns out the house has an unsatisfactory roof.

If the roof leaks and there is evidence inside the house or attic of this leakage, it will probably have to be replaced or repaired before a sale can go through. The cost of applying a new roof depends, first of all, upon the size house and, secondarily, on the slope of the roof. Roofers charge more for roofs that have steep pitches than for more gentle slopes. Roofing is not an overly difficult job. It can be dangerous, however, and requires some heavy lifting to get the shingles up to the roof. Unless you have the time, patience, and basic skills, it is a task that is best left to professionals.

If you hire someone to do the job, you can usually plan on paying from $3,000 to $5,000. You can expect a return of about 77 percent on your investment when you sell the house. In short, roof replacement is a fairly good investment but should only be done if it has to be.

Unless you already have to replace windows for some reason, replacing windows simply for the purpose of increasing the resale value of your house is probably not the best investment you can make. For one reason, window replacement isn't cheap. You can generally plan on spending at least $5,000 to replace the windows in an average house, of which much less than 50 percent will be returned when you sell the house. What you can do, however, is make sure that the windows you have are in good shape. See that they are painted, puttied, and washed. Replace any broken or cracked panes. Be sure that you have serviceable screens and storm windows for each window, if necessary.

Two popular exceptions include garden windows and skylights. Although *garden windows* will not appreciably increase the value of your house, they are attractive and relatively easy and inexpensive (less than $300 for materials) to install. Homeowners in extreme climates should be sure to use double-pane windows, and all homeowners should ensure that the units are properly sealed to prevent leakage around the window. Garden windows provide the additional benefit of making a small kitchen, the room in which the windows are normally installed, seem larger.

While just as popular as garden windows, *skylights* are more costly and difficult to install because holes must be cut into the roof. A typical skylight can cost more than $1,000 to install, including interior finishing, if done by a professional.

You might also want to replace large patio windows and sliding doors, which usually have aluminum frames, because they are not particularly energy efficient and are a security risk. One of the most popular replacements for patio doors and windows is the wooden atrium door. Atrium doors can be expensive, up to $1,000 for the door unit itself. They are sometimes difficult to install, especially if the sliding door taken out is not the same size as the new door being put in. If you are an experienced do-it-yourselfer, however, and if you have someone helping you lift and move the door unit, you should be able to install the door in one day and finish it out the next. Finished atrium doors make a much better impression on home shoppers and are generally considered a better than average investment.

BUYER PREFERENCE

When it comes to exterior siding on a house, the top three alternatives are brick, wood, and stucco. In general, brick seems to be the preferred material, with about half of all home shoppers indicating a preference for it. What is surprising is that the more expensive the house, the greater the desire for brick siding. Wood siding, however, remains the material of choice for about one out of every three shoppers, while stucco is preferred by about one out of every five shoppers.

Exterior color preferences continue to lean towards neutral shades, with white, off-white, tan, beige, and gray being the top choices. Almost half of home shoppers elect white; slightly more than one-third pick tan, beige, or off-white. Fewer than one out of ten shoppers opt for gray, while other colors are singled out even less. Colors used for the trim parallel siding preferences. The trim color preferred by about one out of three buyers is brown, while about one out of four like white. Tan, beige, and off-white trim colors appeal to fewer than one out of every five buyers.

Although most of today's roofs are covered by composite shingles, most of today's shoppers prefer houses with other types of roofing. The roofing material preferred by two out of three buyers is clay tile, even though it cost much more. About one out of every five buyers prefer wooden shakes and shingles, while slightly more than one out of every ten shoppers want composite shingles.

9

Utilities and Appliances

THE FRAME AND STRUCTURAL COMPONENTS OF A HOME ARE often referred to as the skeleton of the house, while the walls, roof, and flooring are called the skin. If one were to carry out this analogy, then the utility functions—electrical service, gas service, and plumbing—might be referred to as the nervous and digestive systems of a house.

When many houses are sold, major appliances like the refrigerator stove, washer/dryer, and hot water heater are often included with the house, especially when built-in appliances are used, Fig. 9-1. While some home buyers might have their own appliances, the special design requirements of a particular house might dictate using the existing appliances.

MECHANICAL SYSTEMS

Utility services, also referred to as mechanical systems, are one of those things that homeowners usually take for granted, at least until something goes wrong. When a light bulb burns out, a circuit breaker trips, a faucet drips, or a drain clogs up, then people get worried. Part of the reason for the anonymity of household utilities is that they are often perceived as being mysterious in both their function and their operation. Most homeowners, for instance, can't really describe the electrical system of their house in either general or specific terms. Unless homeowners install utility systems themselves, are there when they are installed, or have carefully examined the house plans, there is little opportunity for a homeowner to learn the layout and operation of utility systems. Because drains, heating ducts, and electrical lines are hidden

Fig. 9-1. *Built-in kitchen appliances like these are usually left with the house when it is sold (courtesy of Whirlpool Corp.).*

149

within walls and beneath the floor, determining after the fact how a house is laid out isn't easy. The bottom line is that if the utility system is laid out correctly using quality materials, homeowners should only have to worry about utility service on extraordinary occasions.

Living in a house that has unreliable mechanical systems that require constant maintenance can be a real headache; selling that house can prove to be next to impossible. Plumbing problems often mean that walls must be torn out or yards dug up, and home shoppers don't want to buy a house with these upfront deficiencies. Therefore, it is important that you understand the basics of home mechanical systems in general and of your house in particular. You can safely assume that home shoppers will look at and ask questions about the utility services.

ELECTRICAL SYSTEMS

A home electrical system consists of several components—switches, receptacles, electrical boxes, wiring, and breakers. The components that you are most familiar with and use the most are switches that turn the lights on and off. Although there are all kinds of specialty switches used for distinct applications, there are really only about two basic kinds of switches that are commonly used in homes—single-pole and three-way toggle switches.

Single-pole switches are the most common and usually control only a single light. They are marked with two positions (on and off) and, as a rule, have two screw terminals, one for the hot wire and one for the neutral. A *three-way switch*, on the other hand, enables a single light to be controlled from two locations. These are often used in rooms that have two entry doors. Wiring them is more complicated than with single-pole switches, and the switch itself is more expensive to buy. A three-way switch has a single copper-colored terminal and two silver- or brass-colored terminals.

In many homes, *dimmer switches*, which provide variable light intensity, can easily replace existing toggle switches. When a light must be controlled from three locations, *four-way switches* can be used.

Almost as commonly used as switches are *receptacles*, also called *outlets*. Most outlets have two receptacles (called *duplex outlets*), although some outlets (like those located above kitchen cabinets, for instance) have an outlet and a switch. Wires are usually connected to outlets via side-mounted screws or clamps. Most receptacles have two brass-colored terminals for hot wires and two silver-colored screws for neutral wires. A ground wire should be connected to the green-colored screw.

Switches, outlets, lights, and any other point of electrical inter-connection must be made within an *electrical box*. Typically, these boxes are securely fastened to wall studs or ceiling joists. Connecting the various electrical components to each other and to the source of electrical power is the *wiring*. Because of the publicity surrounding the large number of fires caused by aluminum wiring, home shoppers are on the lookout for houses that use this material. If your house has aluminum wiring, be prepared to deal with questions that will undoubtedly be asked about it.

All house wiring eventually is connected to the *service entry box* and its associated *circuit breakers* or *fuses*. When circuit overloads occur, a circuit breaker will trip or a fuse will blow. The main circuit switch is typically rated between 60 and 120 amps, with most household circuit breakers used rated at 15, 20, or 30 amps.

Design Strategies

Many facets of electrical layout and design are governed by local building codes. The first thing you want to be sure of is that your system meets code requirements. This usually means that for every 12 linear feet of wall, there should be at least one duplex receptacle. In some areas of the house—along kitchen cabinets, bathroom vanity, or garage workbenches—you might want outlets as close as 6 feet or less. (In the garage, you can install an outlet in the ceiling to accommodate an automatic garage-door opener.) Table 9-1 provides a guideline for the general electrical requirements of a typical house. Table 9-2 describes how electricity might be distributed throughout a typical house.

The kitchen has special electrical requirements because of the large number of electrical appliances used there. Usually, the kitchen needs two or more 20-amp small appliance circuits. You also need circuits for major appliances, including a 240-volt line for an electric stove, even if you don't plan on using such an appliance (future owners might).

Table 9-1. Typical Electrical Needs of a Standard House

Location	Ceiling Light Fixtures	Wall Switches	Receptacles
Bedroom			
Master	1	1	5
Secondary	1	1	4
Bath			
Master	2	1	1
Secondary	2	1	1
Entry Hall	1	2	3
Living Room	1	2	6
Dining Room	1	2	5
Kitchen	1	2	9
Utility Room	1	1	2

Table 9-2. Home Electrical Distribution System (200-amp Main Circuit Breaker).

Circuit Location	Amount (amps)	Use
Kitchen		
Major Appliances	20	Refrigerator, Freezer
Small Appliances	20	Coffee Maker, Food Processor
Outlets	20	Toaster
Lighting	15	Overhead Light
Oven/Range	30	
Dishwasher	20	
Garbage Disposal	15	
First Floor		
Living/Family Room	15	TV, Stereo
Entry Hall	15	Lighting
Dining Room (see Living Room)		
Bedroom	15	Lighting, Outlets
Bathroom	15	Lighting, Outlets
Laundry Room		
Dryer	30	
Washer/Iron	20	
General Utility		
Water Heater	20	
Air Conditioner	50	
Furnace	20	
Garage	20	Lighting, Door Opener

Light switches should be beside every doorway into a room. If a room does not have an overhead lighting fixture, connect the wall switch so that it controls an outlet that can have a lamp plugged into it. You should also try to have exterior outlets for the outside of the house, usually one in the front yard and one in the back. These will require special waterproof cover plates.

Remodeling Strategies

One of the first things home shoppers will do when entering a room in your house is turn on the lights. If the light comes on quietly and correctly, most buyers will not give the switch or outlet a second thought. If the switch is noisy, the switch plate cover old and dirty, or if the light doesn't function properly, the buyer will become immediately suspicious.

Consequently, it is worth your time to make a quick review of all lights in the house to ensure that they work properly and that the covers are clean and not broken. New single-pole switches usually don't cost much more than a dollar and cover plates about a quarter. Installing new ones, as well as new light bulbs, is well worth the time and effort it takes. New cover plates on both the outlets and switches look clean and up-to-date and convey the impression that the house has been well maintained.

When it comes to items in the house such as light switches and fixtures, home shoppers tend to notice what is missing and simply accept what is present. If there are no outdoor lights, particularly in homes that have a large backyard and patio, buyers will realize that they will have to install some. At the same time, they might notice whether or not there are any exterior outlets, especially in houses that will require electrical gardening tools (hedge trimmers, for instance) to maintain the landscaping.

Older homes often have electrical services that don't meet today's home electrical requirements. If a large house has only a 60-amp fuse box, you might want to upgrade it to 120-amp circuit box, especially if you are going to be in the house for a few years before selling it.

In addition to features such as new cover plates, dimmer switches are popular in master suites, living rooms, and dining rooms. They are a relatively easy and cheap component to install and make a good impression on home shoppers.

PLUMBING SYSTEMS

In theory, plumbing systems are very simple. They basically consist of pipes that bring fresh water into the house, fixtures that control water once it is there, and pipes that drain waste water out of a house. If you've ever had to unclog a drain or repair a frozen water pipe, however, you already know that it isn't quite that simple.

Home shoppers are generally less concerned about the condition of the plumbing system than they are about the condition of the electrical system. The reason for this is simple: while a defective plumbing system can be messy and a nuisance, it can't really catch on fire and burn down the house.

There are a few things home shoppers will look for when evaluating the plumbing system of your house. The first thing is water leaks. A common problem area for water leakage is around the base of a toilet. If your house has this problem, get it fixed before showing the house. At the same time, if there is any remaining traces of water damage caused by previous leaks (water-stained ceiling tiles or flooring, for instance), have it repaired, or it might raise questions concerning the reliability of the plumbing system.

Banging water pipes will also make home shoppers nervous. *Water hammer* is one common type of pipe noise that usually occurs when water is shut off. Although it makes an awful noise, it usually isn't damaging and can be stopped by simply attaching short lengths of vertical, capped pipes to the system. This will provide an air cushion for when the pressurized water is turned off.

When inspecting your house, home shoppers will also turn on the faucets and flush the toilet to check water pressure. If you have the water running in the kitchen or bathroom and flushing the toilet causes a severe loss of pressure, consult a plumber before showing the house.

Another water system component buyers will look at closely is the water heater. If the temperature regulator is turned up to the maximum, yet the water is only moderately hot, you might want to shut down the water heater and drain it to remove sediment that has collected inside the unit.

Remodeling Strategies

There usually isn't much you can or should do about renovating the plumbing of your house unless you have had major problems or are remodeling other parts of the house anyway. What you can do is spruce it up. Before showing your home to potential buyers, replace the plumbing fittings in the kitchen and baths. These fittings usually involve the faucet and knobs for the kitchen and bathroom sinks and in the shower and bathtub. Gleaming new fittings will help make a bathroom and kitchen look up-to-date and, with a minimum of cost and effort (except, perhaps, for a plumber), can really let you show off your house.

HEATING AND COOLING SYSTEMS

The importance of heating and cooling systems to home shoppers depends, to a large degree, on where your house is located. Obviously, home buyers in extremely cold or hot climatic regions will place more importance on these systems than shoppers in more moderate regions. In the northern regions where cold winters and moderate summers are the norm, it is very important to have an efficient, safe, and economical heating system, even a backup system in many cases. In the extreme southern and southwest parts of the country, the winters are usually mild while the summers are long and hot. Here a good cooling system is more important. Throughout the Midwest and on the East Coast where hot, humid summers are followed by very cold winters, both heating and cooling are important.

These days, the most common home heating system is the *thermostatically controlled, forced-air central-heat furnace*, which distributes warm air throughout the house via ducts (pipes). Forced-air furnaces are usually heated by either gas (natural or propane) or oil. Other types of commonly used heating systems include *electric furnaces, heat pumps,* and *hot-water.* Each type has advantages and disadvantages. The two main concerns home buyers have when it comes to heating, however, are convenience and cost. Secondary concerns revolve around cleanliness, noise, and humidity levels. When it comes to cooling the house, central air conditioners (those that use the same ductwork to carry cool air that furnaces use to carry warm air) are much preferred over the more portable window units.

Because furnaces and air conditioners are mechanical devices, they are susceptible to the same type of problems as other machines. Common complaints include squeaky belts and dusty air. These can be minimized by regular preventive maintenance.

Home shoppers will often take a cursory look at the heating and cooling systems, leaving a more in-depth inspection up to professional inspectors. What shoppers will look at, however, is something that has a great impact on the effectiveness of a heating or cooling system—insulation. While heating and cooling units might be foreign to many home shoppers, they can understand insulation. They know whether it is there or not, and they realize the importance of having adequate insulation in a house.

Other than making sure that your heating and cooling system is working and that it is adequate to heat or cool the size of house you have, there isn't a whole lot you can do to spruce it up. Certainly keeping the system clean (ducts, filters, vents, etc.) helps, as will properly servicing it so that it runs quiet. If you are installing a system in a new or remodeled house, select the type of furnace that uses the least expensive type of fuel for where you live. Homeowner's in the Midwest, for instance, will not find an oil-fired furnace particularly attractive because propane and natural gas are usually cheaper in that area.

Remodeling Strategies

When it comes to heating and cooling, the two most common remodeling projects involve installing central air-conditioning and forced-air furnaces. On average, it costs $2,500 to install either a central air-conditioning system or a forced-air furnace. Depending on the area in which you live, the furnace will usually provide a greater return on investment than the cooling system.

One reason air conditioners have less impact in moderate climates is that window unit air conditioners are more commonly used. In these areas, a good (and relatively inexpensive, especially if you are upgrading the electrical system anyway) renovation is to have 220/240-volt electrical outlets located in strategic areas of the house to accommodate the window units.

If you are going to be in the house for a while before selling it and need to install a new furnace, you should probably invest in a super- or high-efficiency furnace. If the house sells right away, you probably won't get back your investment. If you live in the house a few years, however, you'll save a significant amount of money on your monthly utility bills.

It should be mentioned that one of the easiest and least expensive heating and cooling renovations is a simple installation of energy-saving material like caulking and insulation. In many areas of the country, insulation and caulking are dictated by local building codes and must be up-to-code before the house can be sold. An energy-saving upgrade costs about $1,000. As with a furnace, you will recover most of this investment through lower heating and cooling bills if you stay in the house a few years.

One major energy saving renovation is the replacement of existing windows, particularly single-pane units, with tighter, double-pane windows. This is a big job and generally quite expensive (up to $10,000 or more for an average house) even if you do it yourself. And even if you live in the house for several years following the upgrade, you will probably not realize a payback in investment value or lower heating bills. In those extreme climatic areas where windows really make a difference, it is more reasonable to put up exterior storm windows.

Most alternate energy renovations do not pay off when you sell the house in the short-term. A solar-water heating system, for instance, can cost several hundred dollars to install, and only about one out of every four buyers are willing to pay extra for such a system.

Don't forget that a fireplace is considered an alternate energy heating source too. As discussed earlier, they are a very good investment and one of the basic features home buyers look at when evaluating homes. Consequently, they can both pay for themselves as you use them and provide a nice return when you sell the house.

APPLIANCES

Small appliances like coffee makers and toasters have little bearing on a home shopper's decision about whether or not they might buy a particular house. Major appliances that stay with the house do play a part, however. While appliances like refrigerators, washing machines, and hot-water heaters usually won't make or break a house sale, they can provide either the seller or the buyer with a bargaining edge. The seller, for instance, might "throw in" the refrigerator or washing machine if it will help close a deal.

Having a modern kitchen (that is, a kitchen with numerous, new, and convenience-oriented appliances) is not overly important to home shoppers, especially because kitchens are one of the areas in the house that most homeowners remodel within the first year or two of purchasing a house. With this in mind, it is more important to home shoppers that houses have large kitchens, like those shown in Chapter 4, than a modern one. If the floor space is there, they can always add the appliances.

Obviously, hot-water heaters, furnaces, and, in some geographical areas, air conditioners and other such devices are mandatory. Other appliances, especially those used in the kitchen, will enhance a sale. Buyers expect today's kitchens (Fig. 9-2) to have a dishwasher as well as, in many cases, a garbage disposal. Home shoppers who have lived in houses or apartments that have these amenities will expect them. If a kitchen doesn't have conveniences such as these, home shoppers will begin thinking of the trouble and turmoil of a future remodeling job.

For those appliances that are present in a house, built-in or not, buyers will first look for whether or not it works. A garbage disposal that doesn't work when switched on will discourage buyers, not attract them. They will see it as an added expense to deal with later, and it will usually put them on guard when looking through the rest of the house. In the same sense, a clothes dryer might simply appear as another piece of junk that

Fig. 9-2. *Appliances such as dishwashers, microwave ovens, and refrigerators with automatic ice makers/dispensers are now considered the norm, not the exception (courtesy of Whirlpool Corp.).*

will have to be hauled away. Keep in mind that the average life of a typical major home appliance is from 10 to 15 years. Refrigerators built 25 years ago look out of style. Even if they work fine, buyers will view them with skepticism, believing that the appliances are old and can break down at anytime.

Secondary to appliance operation is appearance. Maybe that washing machine works fine even though it is rusty and dented, but buyers won't see that. Instead, they'll see trouble lurking. If plastic laminate is coming unglued on the dishwasher, glue it back on before showing the house to shoppers. If the refrigerator is scratched or nicked, touch it up with matching appliance paint. And if you have to buy a new appliance just prior to selling the house, don't expect to get your money back when you sell the house because appliances just aren't that crucial to buyers. The more expensive the house, however, the more buyers will expect the convenience that modern, built-in appliances provide. The rule of thumb is that "bad" appliances can hurt a sale more than "good" appliances can help it.

BUYER PREFERENCE

Perhaps the major concern that home shoppers have expressed regarding utilities and appliances is the energy source that fuels the appliance. The basic question for shoppers is whether to use gas or electricity.

By far, home buyers prefer gas over electricity for the essential necessities—heating, cooking, water heating, and clothes drying. Almost four out of every five home shoppers have expressed preferences for gas in each of these areas.

Without question, it is useful to have electrical outlets in those areas where gas appliances will be used, the laundry room and kitchen in particular. Gas dryers require a 110/120-volt electrical outlets to turn the drum and provide lights, while a gas stove or oven needs an outlet for clocks, lights, etc. You might want to have 220/240-volt electrical outlets in both the laundry area and kitchen for those future buyers who prefer major electrical appliances instead of gas. It would be a mistake, however, to have 220/240-volt electricity and not have gas stubs in those areas.

If you are faced with the necessity of installing a new heating system in your house, it might be a good idea to install a high-efficiency furnace or gas water heater. It probably isn't a good idea to install a new furnace just to sell the house, however. While some home shoppers indicate that such a feature is important to them, fewer than half view the furnace and water heater as crucial. As with all major appliances, it is more important that they work and appear well maintained. Air conditioners have less impact on resale values in areas like the Pacific Northwest than do furnaces. In the same sense, heating systems have less impact in states like Florida than do air conditioners.

Overall energy efficiency does not rate high on the list of special features home buyers look for, even in extreme climates. The relative importance of energy efficiency is directly tied to the availability and cost of inexpensive energy sources. Over the last few years, energy has been relatively inexpensive. If that situation were to change in the coming years, energy efficiency will be more important to home buyers. Therefore, it is to your advantage to make your home as efficient as possible when it comes to energy.

While features like double-pane windows, heavy insulation, and other energy-saving devices are important to about one out of two shoppers, approach them with caution. What you will find is that the lower the investment you make in these areas, the easier it will be to get a positive return on that investment. You will find expensive features like double-pane windows mean relatively little to buyers, while less expensive features like insulation mean more.

10

Outside the House

THE HOUSE ALONE WON'T SELL YOUR HOME. WHEN EVAL-
uating your house, potential buyers will consider not only the structure
itself, but the yard and features that surround it. In addition to the
landscaping of the yard, some of the important outdoor features that you
need to evaluate include driveways and sidewalks, fences and gates,
patios or decks, greenhouses or sunrooms, and hot tubs or swimming
pools. All of these features contribute to the overall appearance of the
house (Fig. 10-1) and, depending on their presence or condition, can play
a big part in how quickly and at what price your house sells.

LANDSCAPING

Realtors generally agree a house setting on a dry, unkempt yard will
not sell as fast as a similar house surrounded by a neat, tidy yard.
Landscaping is very important to buyers for a number of reasons. For
one thing, most home buyers want an attractive home, and the yard plays
a big part in establishing the look of a particular house. The yard is also
an important recreation area for both those shoppers who have small
children and for those homeowners who like to entertain outdoors. In

Fig. 10-1. *You can showcase the outside of your house by making careful use of fences, walks, gates, decks, spas, and greenhouses (courtesy of Ford Custom Lumber).*

many areas of the country, landscaping also contributes to the energy efficiency of a home. Tall shade trees can significantly cut cooling costs in the hot summer months, while coniferous trees along the north side of the house can cut heating bills in the winter.

These examples all point to the positive side of landscaping. Landscaping can also work against you when selling your home. Recall that in Chapter 2, one homeowner found that his elaborately landscaped yard kept his house on the market for an extra six months because many shoppers didn't want to take on the required yard maintenance. Other yards might be so elaborate that they need professional landscaping on a regular basis, and home buyers might not want to incur this extra cost. In hot or dry climates, home shoppers might not want to take on the additional water bills necessary to keep a fancy yard green.

A yard does not have to be ultrafancy to be attractive, however. A modest assortment of trees, shrubs, flowers, and green grass (Fig. 10-2) will give your house what real-estate agents refer to as *curb appeal,* and potential buyers will have a positive first impression when they see your house. One area of the yard that should definitely have some landscaping is around the foundation of the house. An exposed foundation will give a house a stark, barren appearance. A few shrubs or flowers conveniently placed will enhance your home's curb appeal.

Professional landscaping isn't cheap either. It is quite easy to spend $2,000 to $4,000 on a yard to have someone plant trees and shrubs and

Fig. 10-2. *Landscaping can improve the ''curb appeal'' of a house, even on hillside lots.*

to have decorative sidewalks and small retaining walls built. In moderate areas of the country and with more expensive homes, however, one out of two home shoppers indicate that they are willing to pay for a house that has complete landscaping. In general, you'd be advised to go slow with your landscaping projects and keep them in line with the other yards in your neighborhood.

In a recent survey conducted by National Gardening Association for the Weyerhauser Co., real-estate appraisers indicated that well-maintained and well-designed landscaping added nearly 8 percent to the selling price.

PATIOS AND DECKS

With just about all of today's home buyers, outdoor amenities like decks and patios are important. Buyers who have children want outdoor facilities so that the kids will have a place to play, while many adults like to have someplace to entertain outside when the weather is agreeable. Nearly two out of three home shoppers indicate that decks and patios are an important factor when they evaluate a house.

Earlier sections of this book stressed that the entrance to the outside ideally should be through a family room that, in turn, is located next to the kitchen. This points out that you should design the outside conveniences of a property in conjunction with the house itself.

By far, the most popular outdoor recreation area today is the wood deck, usually redwood or treated lumber (Fig. 10-3). More than one out

Fig. 10-3. *Wooden decks are a good home improvement and, as in this case, can provide level recreational space even on a steep, unaccessible hillside.*

of three buyers prefer wood decks to other common alternatives, such as concrete, brick, or stone patios. Fewer than one out of four shoppers prefer concrete patios. Decks are usually a good investment if they are built solidly and well maintained. As with most home improvements, the more you can do yourself, the greater the return you will ultimately show on your investment. Many lumberyards offer both deck kits and classes on how to assemble them. This is a good alternative even for homeowners who have minimal do-it-yourself skills because the task is fairly straightforward.

If you build the deck yourself, you can expect to spend between $1,000 and $1,500 depending on how elaborate it is. You can also expect a return of about 200 percent on your investment if you spend this much. Having a carpenter build the deck will cost you about $3,500 to $4,000, and you can expect a return on investment of less than 70 percent.

Masonry patios are much less popular with home shoppers and more difficult to maintain for homeowners. (If a board cracks, it can easily be replaced. If concrete settles and cracks, much more work is necessary to repair it.) If you have a choice, opt for the wood deck.

With the exception of flowers or other plants, keep patio and deck features to a minimum. Fewer than one out of five buyers have indicated that they want features such as patio grills, patio roofs, and patio privacy fences.

GREENHOUSES AND SUNROOMS

In moderate and warm climates, decks and patios are popular because they can be used year round. Over the past few years, however, cold-climate inhabitants have been turning (or returning in some cases) to greenhouses and sunrooms (Fig. 10-4). From the home seller's per-

Fig. 10-4. *Although their return on investment isn't always the best, greenhouses and sunrooms are on the rise as home improvements, particularly in colder climates.*

spective, prefabricated sunrooms are an attractive feature because they are relatively inexpensive, at least compared to adding a full room, and they can be added quickly and easily.

More realistically, however, greenhouses/sunrooms are highly personalized, and many experts feel that they don't add much to the value of the house. Some homeowners use an attached greenhouse for its stated purpose; that is, to grow plants indoors. Other people use it as an indoor/outdoor recreation or sitting room and often install spas in the room.

As you might expect, the more you spend on such a job—a typical sunroom addition might cost anywhere from $10,000 to $20,000—the more difficult it wil be for you to get a good return on your investment. In most instances, you will recoup more than one-third of your investment when you sell your house.

FENCES

At least in an urban area, it is hard to think of a house that doesn't have some kind of a fence around the perimeter of the yard. That fence might take many forms, from chain link to wooden picket.

Although many fences serve only a cosmetic purpose, there are many practical reasons for having them, including to serve as boundary identifiers, privacy, security, protection, and sound inhibitors. Certainly, homeowners with pets or small children often want to have fences so that either can be outside without constant supervision.

There are many types of fences, and the type you choose will depend upon the problem you are trying to address. If you have small pets, you might be able to get by with a relatively low chain-link fence. If you are trying to ensure privacy from prying neighbors, you will probably want a tall, solid wood fence or a lattice fence covered with vines. About one out of two home buyers say that rear- and side-yard wood fences are important enough to them that they would pay an extra $1,000 to $2,000 for them.

In terms of home resale, what is important to buyers is that the fence be in good shape. For wooden fences, that means no missing or broken slats and that the fence is freshly painted or stained. One way to ensure that a fence remains in good condition is to use composite or manufactured fencing material. Although such material looks like wood, it is more resistant to moisture and other damage than real wood fencing. In any event, buyers tend to prefer wooden (or woodenlike) fences to metal or chain-link fences.

HOT TUBS AND SWIMMING POOLS

Just about everyone likes hot tubs and swimming pools, but fewer people want to pay for them. That's why conveniences such as these are generally considered poor investments unless you intend on living in the house for a long time. In parts of the country, particularly in areas like Florida, the Southwest, and in southern California, swimming pools are much more common and, therefore, more attractive to buyers. Over the past decade, hot tubs have sprouted in all parts of the country. Nonetheless, you, not the buyer, will pay for the luxury of having a pool or a tub. Fewer than one out of four home buyers indicate that a hot tub is important to them, and fewer than that say a pool is significant.

Hot tubs (Fig. 10-5) are obviously less expensive than swimming pools. You can have a standard hot tub and small deck or gazebo installed for about $4,000. Because most of the cost is in the equipment, you won't save but about $500 if you do the work yourself. In both cases, you'll get back less than 50 percent of your investment if you sell the house since only one out of every ten home buyers say they would pay the extra money for a spa.

Swimming pools are a much bigger job, typically costing at least $15,000. There's really no way a do-it-yourselfer can do the job, especially if it is like the luxurious pool/spa shown in Fig. 10-6. Added to that is the higher costs of maintenance, water bills, and insurance that you must contend with throughout the life of the pool. In warm parts of the country, you might get back 40 percent of your investment; in moderate or cold climates, expect no more than a 30 percent return.

When asked how they feel about swimming pools, only about one out of ten home shoppers polled in California indicate that they would

Fig. 10-5. *Hot tubs are popular, but buyers don't always want to pay too much extra for a house that has one.*

pay the extra $15,000 or $20,000 that a pool would add to the selling price of a house.

For these reasons, swimming pools are generally regarded as one of the worst home improvements that can be made, at least in terms of adding to the resale value of your home.

Fig. 10-6. *Swimming pools and spas do not have a high investment return value, even when they are less elaborate than at this house (courtesy of The Fieldstone Co.).*

11

Homeowner Warranties

FEW PEOPLE WOULD BUY A CAR, TELEVISION SET, CLOTHES dryer, or other such device unless it came with some sort of warranty that reimbursed them in some way if it breaks down shortly after purchasing it. As a homeowner, though, you spend far more money on a house than you would ever think of spending on washing machines or dishwashers, yet you rarely have any guarantee covering structural defects you don't know about when buying the house. What would you do, for instance, if two weeks after you moved into your new house the furnace completely broke down and a repairman told you it needed to be replaced? What typically happens in cases like this are that homeowners are stuck with any repair bills and their only recourse is to sue the builder, developer, or previous owner.

Because of structural and mechanical defects in both new and existing homes, *homeowner warranties* have become quite common over the past decade. Basically a homeowner warranty is an insurance policy that protects the owner of a recently purchased house against specified defects that were unknown when the house was bought. Even when thorough inspections are conducted, defects like furnaces (that is no longer under a manufacturer's warranty) that are about to break down are difficult to detect. In this case, a homeowner warranty might cover the repair of the furnace at little or no cost to the homeowner or seller.

As with any insurance policy, the coverage provided by a homeowner warranty depends on the particular contract. In some cases, the warranty will cover mechanical and structural defects; in other cases, coverage might be limited to one or the other. The thing that is valuable about insured warranties is that they put in writing exactly what is covered and what is not. Having issues in writing eliminates potential bickering between buyer and seller and lets the responsible party get on with rectifying the problem.

If you're not familiar with homeowner warranties, you might wonder where you get one. There are two types of homeowner warranties available. One source is home builders who often provide new-home warranties for those houses they put up. Warranties such as these are usually associated with a specific house, not with an owner, and like assumable mortgages, can be passed on to future buyers as a house is sold. For existing homes, real-estate agencies, particularly nationwide realty chains, often provide a warranty service. In these instances, the buyer sometimes takes out the warranty as a sales incentive.

When they are available, home warranties aren't overly expensive, and for new-home buyers might not cost anything at all. In these instances, builders typically pay for the coverage as part of the cost of the house. Usually a builder pays about $3.00 for every $1,000 of sale price. (In other words, a warranty for a $100,000 home would cost $300.) Sellers or buyers of existing homes usually are faced with a flat fee of about $300.

As with most insurance policies, deductibles (usually ranging from $150 to $200) are common. Figure 11-1 illustrates a typical home warranty agreement, although coverage varies from company to company and from state to state. Most home warranties are transferable to second owners for a small transfer fee, usually not more than $50.

All home warranties aren't the same. Certain ones only provide coverage for up to a year or so, others provide coverage for up to 10 years. Some warranties cover structural and mechanical defects, others cover mechanical and major appliances, and others cover only mechanical defects. New houses in particular are often covered by a ''2-10'' warranty: 2-year coverage for plumbing, electrical, and mechanical systems; and a 10-year protection against structural defects. For specific information about the different types of coverage available, contact one of the warranty suppliers listed at the end of this chapter.

If a home is covered by a warranty and a problem occurs, the homeowner usually only needs to call the insurance provider's service center (most provide toll-free, 24-hour-per-day, 365-days-per-year service) and tell them the problem. The company then contacts a licensed, bonded contractor in the area who calls the homeowner to arrange a repair call. The deductible usually is not more than $35 to $50, depending on individual policies, as described in Table 11-1 under the heading ''Cost with Coverage.''

APPLICATION

PREMIER PROTECTION™

Save time and paperwork, phone-in this application now!
Dial (800) 782-2211

Please print clearly and press firmly.
You are making five copies.

Application
No. **7446535**

American Home Shield of California, Inc.
90 South E Street, Suite 200
Santa Rosa, CA 95404

IMPORTANT: For service call American Home Shield
ONLY: 1-800-642-2471

*American Home Shield will not reimburse for
services performed without its approval.*

FOR DISTRIBUTOR USE ONLY
Dist. Code: ☐☐☐☐ - ☐☐☐☐ - ☐☐☐☐

Applicant is: ☐ Seller ☐ Buyer

SECTION 1

Applicant's Name _____

Property Address _____

City _____ State _____ Zip _____

Listing Expiration Date _____

Applicant's Mailing Address _____
(If different from property address)

City _____ State _____ Zip _____

Applicant's Phone (____) _____

Real Estate Company Name _____

Address _____

City _____ State _____ Zip _____

Telephone (____) _____

Has a buyer been found for this property?
If yes, please complete Section 3 below. ☐ Yes ☐ No

Name of real estate agent filing application

First _____ Last _____

SECTION 2 Cost of Plan and Options Available

Basic Coverage for Home Seller and Home Buyer

☐ **$295.00** For single family dwelling under 4000 square
feet. (For prices on over 4000 square feet and
multiple units, call 800-642-2440)

Coverage Period: Home Buyer's Coverage begins upon close of escrow, provided plan fee is paid to the Company, and continues for one year after close of escrow. If elected and payment agreed to, Optional Listing and Escrow Period Coverage for the Home Seller begins 10 days from receipt and acceptance of application by the Company and continues through the initial listing and escrow period.

NOTICE TO ESCROW COMPANY: If the home seller has elected listing and escrow period coverage, Section 12740 of the Insurance Code requires home warranty companies to collect the basic coverage and option fee plus a pro rata amount of the basic coverage fee at close of escrow. For this contract, such pro rata amount is $.81 per day from effective date of application through day before close of escrow.

Optional Coverages for Home Buyer Only (✓ each coverage desired)

(a) _____ + $ 50.00 Ducted Electric Central Air Conditioning or Evaporative Cooler (Gas Air Conditioning not covered)

(b) _____ + $125.00 Swimming Pool

(c) _____ + $125.00 Spa Only

(d) _____ + $125.00 Common System Swimming Pool with Built-in Spa

(e) _____ + $ 50.00 *Additional* Pool or Spa, if separate (includes Exterior Hot Tub or Whirlpool); Select only if option (b), (c), or (d) has also been selected.

(f) _____ + $125.00 Washer, Dryer and Refrigerator Package

$ _____ **Total of Optional Coverage(s) Selected**

+ $295.00 Basic Coverage

$ _____ **TOTAL**

SECTION 3 Please fill in as soon as home buyer information is available. Mail blue copy (2) to American Home Shield, pink copy (3) to Escrow Company.

Escrow Company _____

Company's Address _____

City _____ State _____ Zip _____

Telephone (____) _____

Escrow Agent's Name _____

Escrow File Number _____

Proposed Closing Date _____

Buyer's Name _____

See reverse side for contract

ELECTION OF COVERAGE:

Choose one of the following by checking the appropriate box *and* signing the signature line below:

☐ **Home Buyer's Coverage Only:** I desire home warranty protection for home buyer and understand coverage begins at close of escrow.

☐ **Home Seller's and Home Buyer's Coverage:** I desire home warranty protection for home buyer *and* listing and escrow period coverage for home seller and instruct escrow holder to withhold $.81 per day, plus fee for basic and optional coverages for home buyer.

Approval _____

CA-A-288-A #90050   Signature _____ Date _____

COPY ONE –
Upon acceptance of coverage,
Mail immediately to
American Home Shield
P.O. Box 280
Pleasanton, CA 94566
(Envelope attached)

Fig. 11-1. *Sample home warranty agreement (courtesy of American Home Shield of California, Inc.).*

A. COVERAGE

American Home Shield of California, Inc. (the "Company") will, during the coverage period of the home buyer's (and, if applicable, home seller's) contract, repair or replace the covered systems and appliances in accordance with the terms and conditions set forth herein.

1. This contract outlines the types of coverages available. For the specific coverage on your home, see the reverse side of this contract. Please read your contract carefully. Coverage includes only the items stated as covered (subject to certain limitations and conditions) and excludes all others.

2. This contract covers only single family resale dwellings (including manufactured housing) under 4,000 square feet, unless additional plan fee is paid.

3. Coverage is provided only if the covered item is located within the perimeter of the main foundation of your home or garage, and is in good working order at the start of coverage.

4. The following are not covered for the first 30 days after close of escrow for the home buyer (and if coverage is provided, home seller): a). Malfunction or improper operation due to rust or corrosion of appliances, heating and/or air conditioning systems or pools/spas. b). Collapsed ductwork.

B. COVERAGE PERIOD

Home buyer's coverge begins upon close of escrow, and continues for one year after close of escrow, provided plan fee is paid to the Company. If elected and payment agreed to, optional listing and escrow period coverage for the home seller begins 10 days from receipt and acceptance of application by the Company and continues through the initial listing and escrow period.

C. SERVICE CALLS

1. The Company has the sole right to select the technician to perform service. **The Company will not reimburse for services performed without its approval.**

2. The homeowner or his agent (including tenant) must notify the Company of malfunction of covered equipment by calling 800-642-2471 as soon as the problem is discovered. For your convenience we accept service calls 24 hours a day, 7 days a week.

3. Service calls will be dispatched by the Company to a service technician within 36 hours during normal business hours and 48 hours on weekends and holidays. Efforts will be made to expedite service in emergencies.

4. Notice of malfunction must be given to the Company prior to the expiration of the plan.

5. The homeowner is responsible for paying $35 per trade call (or the actual cost of service, whichever is less) when the technician arrives at the home. Failure to pay the trade call fee will result in suspension of coverage until such time as fee is paid. At that time coverage will be reinstated but the coverage period will not be extended.

6. If a repair made under this contract should fail, the Company offers a courtesy recall period of 90 days on parts and 30 days on labor, without an additional trade call fee.

D. SPECIFIC DESCRIPTION OF COVERAGES

BASIC COVERAGE AVAILABLE FOR HOME BUYER AND (IF APPLICABLE) HOME SELLER
TRADE CALL FEE $35.00 (or actual cost of service, whichever is less)

1. PLUMBING SYSTEM:
COVERED: Leaks and breaks in water, drain, gas, vent or waste lines, except if caused by freezing • Toilet tank mechanisms, toilet tanks and bowls will only be replaced with builder's standard • Toilet wax ring seals • Toilet flanges • Diverter valves, angle stops, risers and gate valves • Permanently installed sump pumps • Built-in bathtub whirlpool motor and pump assemblies • $500 limit during coverage period for concrete or slab-encased plumbing, water, drain, gas, vent or waste lines.
NOT COVERED: Stoppages • Faucets, including shower and tub valves • Fixtures • Sinks and bathtubs • Shower enclosures and base pans • Caulking or grouting • Septic tanks • Water softeners • Pressure regulators • Excessive water pressure • Inadequate water supply • Water flow restrictions caused by rust, corrosion or chemical deposits • Toilet lids and seats • Sewage ejector pumps • Leaks/breaks caused by freezing • Holding or storage tanks • Saunas or steam rooms.

2. EXTERIOR WELL PUMP:
COVERED: All components and parts of well pump utilized for main dwelling use only. Except
NOT COVERED: Well casings • Pressure tanks • Piping or electrical lines leading or connecting to pressure tank and main dwelling • Holding or storage tanks • Redrilling of wells.

3. WATER HEATER:
COVERED: All components and parts. Except
NOT COVERED: Circulating pumps • Solar water heaters • Solar components • Holding or storage tanks.

4. HEATING SYSTEM OR BUILT-IN WALL UNITS: (If main source of heat to home)
COVERED: All components and parts, including regulation of burners. (Heat exchangers) [combustion chambers] are covered for the home buyer only. $500 limit during coverage period for concrete or slab-encased radiant heating lines). Except
NOT COVERED: Baseboard casings • Oil storage tanks • Portable units • Filters • Electronic air cleaners • Humidifiers • Solar heating systems • Heat lamps. No coverage is provided for heat exchangers (combustion chambers) during the listing and escrow period. $1500 limit during coverage period for hot water or steam circulating heating systems.

5. DUCTWORK:
COVERED: All ductwork leading from the unit to the point of attachment at registers and grilles. Except
NOT COVERED: Registers and grilles • Insulation • Concrete-encased ductwork • Asbestos insulated ductwork • Collapsed ductwork is not covered for the home seller or for the first 30 days after close of escrow for the home buyer.

6. ELECTRICAL SYSTEM:
COVERED: All components and parts including built-in exhaust fans. Except
NOT COVERED: Fixtures • Door bells • Alarms • Intercoms • Inadequate wiring capacity • Power failure or surge • Garage door openers.

BUILT-IN KITCHEN APPLIANCES:
(Portable dishwasher or trash compactor left by the previous owner will be covered only if make and color are noted on the application)

7. DISHWASHER:
COVERED: All components and parts. Except
NOT COVERED: Racks • Baskets • Rollers.

8. GARBAGE DISPOSAL:
COVERED: All components and parts.

9. MICROWAVE OVEN - BUILT-IN ONLY:
COVERED: All components and parts, including touch-tone panels. Except
NOT COVERED: Interior linings • Door glass • Clocks • Shelves • Portable or counter-top units • Rotisseries • Meat probe assemblies.

10. RANGE/OVEN/COOKTOP:
COVERED: All components and parts, including timers and self-cleaning mechanisms. Except
NOT COVERED: Clocks (unless they affect the function of the oven) • Meat probe assemblies • Rotisseries • Racks • Handles • Knobs • Sensi-heat burners will only be replaced with standard burners.

11. TRASH COMPACTOR:
COVERED: All components and parts. Except
NOT COVERED: Lock and key assemblies • Removable buckets.

OPTIONAL COVERAGE AVAILABLE FOR HOME BUYER ONLY AFTER CLOSE OF ESCROW
[Available to home buyer only when the additional premiums are paid at close of escrow]
TRADE CALL FEE $35.00 (or actual cost of service, whichever is less)

12. DUCTED ELECTRIC CENTRAL AIR CONDITIONING OR EVAPORATIVE COOLER:
COVERED: All components and parts. Except
NOT COVERED: Gas air conditioning systems • Condenser casings • Registers and grilles • Filters • Electronic air cleaners • Window or wall units • Water towers.

13. POOL AND/OR SPA EQUIPMENT: (Both pool and spa [including exterior hot tub and whirlpool] are covered if they utilize common equipment. If they do not, only pool is covered, unless additional premium is paid.)
COVERED: All components and parts of the heating, pumping and filtration system. Except
NOT COVERED: Pool sweeps • Pool sweep motors • Lights • Liners • Concrete-encased or underground electrical, plumbing or gas lines • Cleaning equipment • Structural defects • Solar equipment.

WASHER/DRYER/REFRIGERATOR PACKAGE

14. CLOTHES WASHER:
COVERED: All components and parts. Except
NOT COVERED: Plastic mini-tubs • Soap dispensers • Filter screens • Knobs and dials • Damage to clothing.

15. CLOTHES DRYER:
COVERED: All components and parts. Except
NOT COVERED: Venting • Lint screens • Knobs and dials • Damage to clothing.

16. KITCHEN REFRIGERATOR:
COVERED: All components and parts including integral freezer unit. Except
NOT COVERED: Racks • Shelves • Icemakers, ice crushers, beverage dispensers and their respective equipment • Interior thermal shells • Freezers which are not an integral part of the refrigerator • Food spoilage.

E. LIMITATIONS ON LIABILITY

1. The Company is only responsible for repair or replacement of covered systems and appliances that malfunction due to normal wear and tear. Company is not responsible for repair or replacement of any system or appliance which malfunctions as a result of:
   a. A condition which constitutes a violation of current building or similar codes.
   b. Improper installation, design or previous repair.
   c. Failure to clean or generally maintain.
   d. Alteration or modification from the manufacturer's original specifications.
   e. The inadequacy or lack of capacity of any component in the home. The Company will not upgrade due to lack of capacity or inadequate design.
   f. Misuse or abuse, missing parts, structural changes, freezing, fire, electrical failure or surge, water damage, lightning, mud, earthquake, storms, accidents, pest damage, or acts of God.

2. The Company is not liable for consequential or secondary damages resulting from the failure of a covered item, nor failure to provide service due to conditions beyond its control, such as but not limited to, delays in obtaining parts or equipment, or labor difficulties.

3. The Company is not responsible for the repair of cosmetic defects.

4. The Company has the sole right to determine whether a malfunction will be corrected by repair or replacement. Parts and replacements will be of similar or equivalent quality or efficiency to those being replaced (except for toilet tanks and bowls which will only be replaced with builder's standard, and sensi-heat burners which will only be replaced with standard burners). The Company will not upgrade and is not responsible for matching color or brand.

5. The Company reserves the right to require a second opinion at its expense.

6. When performance of service is affected by building or similar codes so that restoration to original condition is not permitted and/or requires more costly material or additional expense, the Company has no obligation for the additional cost. When corrections of code violations are required prior to performance of service, the homeowner is responsible for making corrections and the Company has no obligation to perform until the corrections are made.

7. The Company is not responsible for providing access to or closing access from any covered item. Except
   a. The Company will provide access to concrete or slab-encased water, drain, gas, vent, waste, or radiant heating lines but repair is subject to a $500 limitation during coverage period.
   b. The Company will provide access to other plumbing, gas, heating or electrical lines but will only restore the opening to rough finish condition.
   c. Under no circumstances is the Company responsible for restoration of such items as wall coverings, floor coverings, cabinets, countertops, tiling, paint and the like.

8. Where replacement equipment of identical dimensions is not generally available, the Company is responsible for providing installation of like quality equipment but is not responsible for the cost of construction or carpentry made necessary by different dimensions.

9. Electronic or computerized energy management or convenience systems are not covered.

10. Coverage will only be provided as long as the property is utilized for residential, and not commercial, purposes.

11. If this plan relates to a multiple unit dwelling, there only is coverage of items contained within the confines of each individual unit. Common areas and facilities are excluded from coverage.

F. MISCELLANEOUS

MULTIPLE UNITS AND INVESTMENT PROPERTY

1. The Company's liability under this contract is limited to a single family dwelling unless contract is amended by the Company to include multiple units, contained in one building, and owned by homeowner named in the contract.

2. Coverage for the home seller is not available on dwellings over four units or on properties processed through the Multiple Unit Division.

LEASE OPTIONS

Coverage on lease options is available for the lessee only, and begins upon payment of plan fee and receipt of application by the Company. Coverage continues for one full year from that date.

RENEWALS

This contract may be renewed at Company's option and where permitted by state law. In that event, homeowner will be notified of the prevailing rate and terms of renewal.

In general, Table 11-1 describes commonly covered mechanical items in the house. For items like the plumbing system, warranties usually cover leaks in the gas or water lines, toilet-tank mechanisms, faucets, pressure tanks, pumps, traps, etc. Electrical systems might include repair to the service panel, wiring, receptacles, switch boxes and switches, and outlets.

Table 11-1. Typical Costs and Coverage for Mechanical Items.

Item Covered	Repair	Repair Cost	Cost with Coverage
Plumbing	Replace 10 feet of line	$135	$0-$35
Water Heater	Replacement (30-50 gal.)	$165	$50
Central Air	Freon leaks	$50-$500	$35-$50
Conditioner	Compressor (3-5 tons)	$600-$1200	$0-$35
	Condenser Unit	$1200-$1500	$0-$35
Range/Oven	Cooktop Replacement	$250-$500	$0-$35
	Oven Replacement	$425-$1400	$0-$35
Garbage Disposal	Replacement	$100-$200	$35-$50
Dishwasher	Replacement	$300-$600	$0-$35
Electrical System	Service panel	$450-$1300	$35-$50

The sorts of things that are typically not covered by home warranty policies include light fixtures, intercoms, stereos, portable heating or cooling units, alarm systems, and solar heating systems.

While the general consensus is that home warranties are a good investment for homeowners, the question home sellers are most concerned with is whether or not home warranties help sell their house. According to real-estate companies and agents, warranties do add value to a house. In general, they say that a home covered by a warranty has a higher value and sells faster than comparable homes that are not covered by guarantees. For example, if two similar homes in the same neighborhood come up for sale at about the same time, say agents, the house that is covered by a homeowner warranty generally sells quicker and at a higher price than the other. So the answer to the question is yes, home warranties do provide buyers with incentives to choose one house over another and can provide sellers with a real edge over competing homes. In fact, a recent Gallup poll showed that eight out of ten adults surveyed considered a home warranty to be an important part of the real-estate transaction.

More specifically, a relatively recent survey conducted in Chicago showed that over a 6-month period, houses covered by home warranties sold about 60 percent faster than those that were not covered by warranties. Furthermore, houses covered by a warranty had an average selling price over $2,000 (or roughly 2 percent) higher than uncovered homes. This isn't a bad investment for home sellers, especially considering that the policies generally cost less than $300 each. Currently in California, about 36 percent of all homes sold are covered by warranties of one kind or another.

NEW HOME WARRANTIES

According to the National Association of Home Builders, over 90 percent of the new homes in the country are covered by a home warranty of one kind or another. In fact, nearly 2 million homes nationwide have been covered by a 10-year warranty provided by the Home Owners Warranty Corp. (Washington, DC). There are commonly three types of warranties that buyers are provided with when buying a new home: an insured warranty, an expressed written warranty, and an implied warranty. A deductible or other fee might be required.

A typical *insured warranty* is a written policy issued by an insurance company that provides coverage against defects in workmanship and material for up to one year, coverage for mechanical system up to two years, and coverage for structural defects (faulty foundation, etc.) for up to 10 years. The one thing about an insured warranty is that it is a written contract that details what is covered and what is not.

An *expressed written warranty*, on the other hand, usually has a much shorter duration, often covering no more than a year. Most often, the warranty states that the builder will return at two specified times within the first year after you move into the house and will repair any defects you find during that time.

Finally, an *implied warranty* isn't necessarily anything in writing but is the collective guidelines established by laws and court rulings that let the buyer assume that he or she has certain rights and that the builder or seller has certain responsibilities. If something goes wrong with your house, the buyer's recourse is usually to take to court the party he feels is responsible.

Builders are rarely required to provide home warranties. They usually do so at their own discretion. Neither is there anything that says a developer has to cover all of his or her homes with a warranty. In special cases, particularly when custom homes have been involved, builders shy away from offering warranties.

EXISTING HOME WARRANTIES

As was stated earlier, the most common warranties for existing homes are available from real-estate contracts. In other words, those real-estate agencies that do provide warranty services only do so for their clients.

Existing home warranties typically are limited to the mechanical aspects of a house—the heating system, the cooling system, and the major appliances. In many instances, an inspection is required by the insurance company carrying the policy. Either the buyer or seller can pay for the warranty, although sellers can use it as an incentive.

Usually, the home buyer is only required to pay a trade service call (deductible) for repair or replacement of covered items. Typical coverage usually lasts for a year after the close of the sale. The seller's coverage is most often in place during the initial listing period. If something breaks during the listing period, the seller pays the deductible. In most states, sellers do not pay for coverage during the listing period, and the contract fee for buyer's and seller's coverage is not due until the home is sold.

If nothing else, a warranty will help assure the buyer that you, as the seller, aren't trying to hide anything and that will go a long way toward helping the buyer feel good about your house. Many home buyers, especially first-time buyers, are nervous when it comes to spending the money required to buy a house, and anything you can do to reassure them will be to your benefit.

A warranty might help spare you from possible litigation, even several years after you sell the house. Within the past couple of years, there have been several instances where sellers have been sued for defects even though several years have passed since they sold the house. A warranty can show good faith, differentiate your house from others on the market, and possibly relieve you of any responsibility.

HOME WARRANTY COMPANIES

American Home Shield Corp.
90 South E St.
Suite 200
Santa Rosa, CA 95404
(800) 782-2211

Electronic Realty Associates, Inc.
4900 College Blvd.
Shawnee Mission, KS 66201
(800) 255-9405

Guaranteed Homes, Inc.
3500 South Service Rd.
Suite 6
Lake St. Louis, MO 63367
(800) 325-8144

Homeowners Association of America, Inc.
6365 Taft St.
Suite 2000
P.O. Box 9200
Hollywood, FL 33084
(800) 327-9787

Realty World/Realsafe
12500 Fair Lakes Circle
Suite 300
Fairfax, VA 22033
(703) 631-9300

United One Home Protection Corporation
2020 Assembly St.
Columbia, SC 20201
(800) 521-4736

12

Home-Showing Strategies

So FAR, THIS BOOK HAS FOCUSED ITS ATTENTION ON LONG-range strategies that will make your house more attractive to potential home buyers. There are, however, short-term steps you can take towards the same end. Some of these measures involve gathering pertinent information that will answer many questions the buyer might have about the house. Other measures involve preparing the house so that it looks attractive.

THE INFORMATION PACK

You'll find that many questions commonly asked by realtors and shoppers can be answered in a single, easily assembled package of information. As you gather the information, you might want to present it in a folder. You also might want to prepare duplicate information packs so that serious shoppers can take the information with them.

What sort of information should you include in the pack? For starters, provide a map or sketch of the neighborhood that identifies local amenities. You can, for instance, identify nearby schools, grocery stores, pharmacies, and parks on the map.

The information pack could also contain a description of the house, perhaps even a photocopied picture of it. Include approximate room sizes and any special features that might be particularly appealing to buyers. This can include the age and warranty expiration date of heating and cooling systems or major appliances or the amount of insulation.

Another useful bit of information is the cost of utilities over a year's time. It shouldn't be necessary to have all of your receipts at hand. Instead, provide a ledger sheet with month-by-month utility expenses. You can include copies of a few monthly receipts, especially if they show that the house was easy to heat during cold months.

Finally, indicate whether or not the house is covered under a home-owner's warranty. Also tell whether your low-cost mortgage can be assumed.

HOW TO SHOW YOUR HOME

Your house should look its best—both inside and outside—anytime it is shown to a prospective buyer. Never forget that first impressions are lasting. When shoppers pull up in front of your house, they will immediately begin deciding whether or not they like it. There are several things you can do to make the house more engaging during the showing process.

There's no question that the best showcase for any home that is for sale is the weekend open house, and real estate agents generally agree that your chances of selling faster and for a higher price are better when you hold an open house. For one thing, the home is open at a time that is convenient for shoppers, and they can examine it at a leisurely pace. From the seller's perspective, open houses provide you with important feedback on how buyers perceive your house. According to some real-estate agents, the odds are 70 to 30 in favor of selling a home by showing it at an open house.

When you want to make an immediate good impression, start with the landscaping. Make sure the lawn is mowed on a regular basis. Not only is a weedy lawn unattractive, but it makes the entire house look run down and unkempt. If you have already vacated the house and can't mow the yard yourself, arrange to have it mowed and have your real-estate agent check that it is. If there is any refuse in the yard, get it cleaned up. Wherever you have sidewalks, be sure that the borders are neatly edged and, if there are flower beds, make sure they are tilled and weeded. In a recent nationwide poll of more than 400 real-estate brokers conducted for ERA Real Estate, a full 100 percent said that the ''sale-ability'' of every house can be improved by exterior landscaping betterments.

As the buyer approaches the house, he or she will be greeted by the front door. Be sure it is clean and, if necessary, freshly painted. If necessary, replace the front-door light fixture and doorbell button. Even little things like new house numbers can make a difference.

Once inside the house, be sure the house is clean and tidy, particularly the kitchen and bathroom. In the ERA Real Estate poll just mentioned, 82 percent indicated that a general house cleaning prior to showing was the most important short-term improvement a house seller could make. Among the specific items you can pay attention to are cleaning carpets, tidying up closets, and touching up the paint. About one out of three agents advise home sellers to replace or add carpeting.

Open the drapes and shades so that the sunlight can illuminate and warm the house, and make it appear more cheerful. However, this means that the windows should be kept clean. If the walls are damaged or dirty (particularly around light switches and doorknobs), it will pay off in the long run to paint or repaper. If switch cover plates are old, dirty, cracked, or painted over, replace them with new plates.

Buyers will not be impressed if the doorknob comes off in their hand as they turn the knob to enter a room. Make all necessary minor repairs to loose knobs, sticking doors and windows, warped cabinet drawers, and so on. If any electrical switches or outlets don't work, have them repaired by an electrician.

If the bathroom or kitchen have leaky faucets, either repair them or have them repaired. Dripping water can discolor sinks and suggest that the plumbing is faulty. Repair all caulking around the bathtub, showers, and countertops. Cabinets can be enhanced by replacing existing knobs and pulls with new ones, and new towel racks, soap dishes, toilet seat, and medicine cabinet can spruce up a bathroom.

Remove all clutter from the rooms, closets, attic, basement, and especially the stairs. For one thing, organized, uncluttered closets and rooms will appear larger. The same goes for the attic, basement, and other storage areas. If you have to dispose of furniture and furnishing when you sell the house, don't wait. Go ahead and get rid of the excess baggage before showing it.

You can enhance a buyer's impression of your house by a few subtle techniques as well:

☐ In the fall or winter, have a fire going in the fireplace, although don't let the house overheat. In warmer seasons, fill the firebox and stack wood in the fireplace, ready to be lit.

☐ Do some baking in the kitchen prior to showing the house. The smell of freshly baked pasteries or bread is especially pleasant.

☐ Some smells are offensive. If you have pets in the house, clean and deodorize the carpets.

☐ Stereo music softly playing in the background can also be relaxing. Avoid a blaring radio or television, which is distracting.

☐ A bouquet of fresh-cut flowers can add to the positive impression you are trying to make.

When the realtor shows up with a prospective buyer, it is usually best if you excuse yourself from the house if possible. Your presence might constrain the buyer from asking pointed questions of the salesperson. If you must be there, try not to have too many additional people in the house because shoppers might feel they are imposing on a family gathering. At the same time, avoid having children or pets running around the house while it is being shown. Whatever you do, don't discuss the terms, possession, or other factors with the shopper; leave that to the salesperson.

Glossary

Glossary

abandonment—The release of a claim to a piece of property.

abatement—A reduction in amount.

abstraction—A method of property valuation whereby the indicated value of an improvement is deducted from the sale price.

abstract of title—A history of the title to a particular property, identifying the rights, liabilities, transfers, and proof of ownership.

acceleration clause—A section of a contract stating that the balance becomes payable immediately when certain conditions are met.

accrue—To gradually increase in value.

act of God—An accident caused by an unpredictable and exceptional natural force (floods, tornados, etc.).

actuary—A person who calculates risks and rates for an insurance company.

adjusted cost—The value of a property that is equal to the original cost plus any improvements, less the depreciation.

after acquired clause—A condition in a contract stating that all assets acquired after a mortgage are subject to that mortgage.

age life depreciation—A method of estimating the depreciation of a house based on the building's expected life.

air-dried lumber—Lumber that has dried without the aid of a kiln. The moisture content in the lumber is in equilibrium with the relative humidity in the air. *See* kiln-dried.

amortize—To pay off a loan.

appraised value—The market value of a house as established by a qualified assessor.

appurtenance—Anything attached to the land that is part of a property.

assessed value—A percentage of the appraised value; used for tax purposes.

attorney's lien—An encumbrance against a property given by the courts upon judgment in cases in which a lawyer has gained an award on behalf of a client.

balloon mortgage—A mortgage with a large final payment.

baseboard—Trim used along the base of an interior wall.

basis—The value of a property for income tax purposes; most often computed by figuring the original cost plus any capital improvements less the accrued depreciation.

betterment—Any improvement to a property that is considered a capital asset and that increases the value.

bill of sale—A legal document that transfers ownership of any personal property.

book value—The value of a property determined by the cost of asset plus improvements less accrued depreciation.

broker—A person who, for some sort of compensation, acts for another person in a real-estate transaction.

broker-to-salesman contract—A document that details the relationship between a broker and a salesperson.

building codes—Legal standards set by local governments that define specifications for virtually all phases of the construction process. Local codes are usually variations of national codes (Uniform Building Codes) and are monitored by municipal building or planning departments, which send building inspectors to check construction projects.

building permit—A document granted by municipal building authorities that allows you to begin building.

CAD—Acronym for Computer-Aided Design, the process of using a computer to help lay out and write specifications for a kit house.

capital gain—The profit received on the sale of a property.

carryover clause—A stipulation in an exclusive listings that protects a broker beyond the expiration date of a commission.

certificate of title—A nonbinding written description of the condition of a title.

chattle mortgage—A loan agreement in which the lender owns the property until the loan is paid off.

clause—An amendment to a contract.

clearance—A report by a qualified pest-control inspector that indicates a house is free from termites and other pests.

clear title—Ownership of any property that is free of mortgages, liens, etc.

closed mortgage—A mortgage that cannot be paid off early.

closing costs—A fee based on a percentage of the loan and paid to the loan company at the time a contract is signed.

closing, loan—The act of signing a contract and other legal documents with a lender so that a loan can be granted.

commission—A real-estate agent's earnings (usually a percentage of the selling price) in negotiating a transaction.

compound interest—Proceeds based on the original investment and the earlier earned interest from it.

construction loan—A relatively short-term loan used to buy materials and pay for labor to build a house. Construction loans are usually granted from 6 to 12 months. Sometimes called a *commercial loan*.

contingency—A condition placed on the sale of a house.

contractor—A person who signs an agreement to perform a certain job. Contractors are generally licensed by a state government. *See* general contractor; subcontractor.

corner lot appraisal—An estimation of the value of a corner lot, which generally assumes greater worth than a noncorner lot. Methods used to estimate the value include the Baltimore Method, Zangerle Curve, and Bernard Rule.

cost analysis—The process of determining the value of a parcel of land. There are two cost-analysis methods: the building cost methods and the comparable sales method.

cost breakdown—An item-by-item analysis of the cost of a house.

covenant—A special agreement between a seller and buyer of land.

decking—The part of the house that covers roof or floor frame, usually made of plywood. Also called sheathing.

decrement—Loss in value.

deed—A legal document that, when executed and delivered properly, transfers the title of real estate.

defeasance—A clause in a deed that, under certain conditions, renders the deed void.

design notebook—A catalog you compile that lists all of the available features you might want a home to have.

dimensional lumber—Structural lumber referred to by size or dimensions, i.e., 1 × 4s, 2 × 6s, etc.

discount—To sell a note for less than its stated value.

earnest money—A deposit made by the buyer to the seller.

easement—Rights of land used by individuals or entities that do not own the land.

elevation—A drawing that shows the way an exterior wall of a house would look when viewed straight on. A house normally can be seen from four elevations.

equity—The difference between how much a house is worth and how much you owe on it.

escrow—Money held by a third party, usually a mortgage company, until all terms of a contract are met.

estimate—A preliminary view of the value of real estate.

exclusive agency listing—A document giving an individual agent the right for a specified time to sell a property.

exterior walls—The outer walls of a house.

first deed of trust—A trust deed that has been recorded before all others and that is first in lien.

fixtures—Items attached to a property that are considered part of that property and that cannot be removed.

floor plan—An approximate graphic description of a house.

footing—Poured concrete that supports the foundation. The footing is usually wider than the foundation, beneath the frost line, and typically from 6 to 12 inches thick.

footing pads—Footings for piers or pillars.

foreclosure—Legal proceedings occuring when a loan company takes possession of a house because the owner has not made payments.

foundation—The vertical perimeter wall that evenly carries the weight of the house to the ground and supports the structure; usually constructed of concrete blocks or poured concrete and considered one of the most critical parts of the building process; usually located partially below the ground level.

framing—The process of erecting, but not covering, the floor, walls, and roof of a house.

front foot—A measurement of property based on a strip of land along the front of the property. That strip consists of 1 foot of frontage and extends the depth of the property.

gable—The pitched end of a house.

gambrel—A double-pitched roof in which one slope is broken by another.

general contractor—The on-site job manager who must ensure that the project runs on schedule.

grading, lumber—Determining and identifying the quality, strength, and characteristics of structural lumber.

hidden amenities—Beneficial conditions that are not noticed at once, but that enhance the property value.

hip—An external angle formed by the meeting of two sides of a roof.

homestead—A house that is protected by law against stipulated debts.

insurable title—A title that can be insured by a title insurance company.

interim financing—A short-term loan.

jamb—One of the sides of a framed opening.

joist—A board or timber that is set "on-edge" to support the floor or roof.

kiln-dried lumber—Lumber that has moisture removed by drying in a kiln (or oven). Kiln-dried lumber is usually much more uniform in its moisture content (about 19 percent) than air-dried lumber.

letter of credit—A document issued by a bank that allows the person named in the letter to draw a certain amount of money from another bank.

lien—Any debt against a property that has been registered with the county clerk.

listing—A contract between a property owner and a real-estate agent authorizing the agent to perform specified service for the property owner.

loan fee—A charge made by a lending institution to cover the cost of processing loan documents. *See* points.

market value—The price at which a seller is willing to sell his property.

mechanic's lien—A legal lien on a property issued for labor or materials used to improve the property.

mortgage—A loan against a property in which the property itself is used as collateral.

mortgage note—Evidence of a debt.

mortgage contract—Security for a debt.

multiple listing—A real-estate listing taken by a member of a multiple listing service. Such a service consists of an association of agents whose members circulate property listings.

note—An agreement made in writing.

obligated room—A room you must pass through to get to another.

on center—Referring to measurements from center to center of parallel boards.

open-end mortgage—A mortgage contract that lets the borrower obtain additional money after the loan has been reduced. At that time, the contract does not need to be rewritten.

open listing—A listing that says the first agent to obtain a buyer will get the commission.

overimprovement—An improvement that generally will not provide a good return on investment.

panelized—A construction method based upon the placement and erection of factory-built wall sections.

partition—An interior wall.

perc test—A test to determine the ability of the soil to absorb discharged wastewater.

pier and beam—Of or referring to a foundation that consists of individual vertical piers connected by horizontal beams which support the floor system.

pitch, roof—The slope of a roof.

plan check—The process in which the building department inspects the construction plans prior to granting a building permit.

plan view—A drawing of a structure from above looking down.

plot plan—A graphic description of a parcel of land that is usually compiled by a licensed surveyor.

points—The amount lending institutions charge for providing mortgages; one point is equal to 1 percent of the sum borrowed.

post-and-beam—Of or referring to a construction framing technique in which large timbers are used as vertical members (the posts) and are then connected by large horizontal members (the beams).

prepayment penalty—An additional charge when a note is paid off before it is due.

prime contractor—The job-site manager who usually hires subcontractors. *See* general contractor.

private restrictions—*See* covenant.

promissory note—A contract that specifies a promise to pay a specified amount of money at a specified future date and time.

public restrictions—*See* zoning.

quiet title action—A lawsuit brought in order to determine a clear title to property.

quit claim—A statement that says there are no debts against a property.

quote—A guaranteed price made in writing in advance.

recording—Filing any papers involving the property title into the public record.

right of access—Legal permission to enter a property.

rough-in—The initial installation of utilities, plumbing, electricity, etc.

second mortgage—A second loan, usually smaller, that is taken out on a home from a second source.

setback requirement—The minimum distance a structure must be from a property line.

sheathing—*See* decking.

shiplap—Of or referring to exterior siding in which one bottom edge is thinner than the top. Bottom edges then overlap the top edges as each course is applied.

simple interest—Interest calculated only on the original principal.

square—100 square feet or three bundles of roofing material.

stucco—An exterior wall finish that consists of cement, sand, lime, and water, and that is held in place by reinforcement wire.

subcontractor—A building specialist hired to complete a single, limited phase of the construction process.

subfloor—Decking material that is nailed to the floor joists but eventually will be covered by a finished floor.

subordination clause—A clause in a contract that subordinates all interest in a property to the claims of another party.

surety—A person who guarantees the performance of another.

take-off—The process of compiling a list of building materials. Sometimes referred to as a schedule.

take-out loan—*See* mortgage.

termite shield—A sheet-metal shield that rests between the foundation and sill to prevent termites from coming in contact with wood.

title—Ownership legally recognized by the county clerk.

title insurance—A special insurance policy that protects the holder against losses because of an inaccurate title.

title search—A review of a property deed to identify any liens, claims, taxes, or assessments against it.

topographical plat—A drawing that illustrates the contours and surface of a plot of land.

trim—Finish material.

variance—An exception to a zoning rule.

voucher-control service—A method of paying subcontractors and suppliers in which the bank pays the debt from an escrow account once the bank is satisfied the work is complete and acceptable.

warranty deed—A deed containing a covenant of guarantee in which the grantor of the deed ensures that the title is free from defects and that the property is unemcumbered except as expressed.

wrap-around mortgage—An agreement in which the borrower takes on a second mortgage without refinancing the first mortgage.

zoning—Of or referring to local regulations that govern the use and application of specific land areas.

Index

Index